THE NEW
MAGICIAN'S MANUAL

Tricks and Routines with Instructions for
Expert Performance by the Amateur

By WALTER B. GIBSON

With Drawings by
WILLIAM H. HANNA

Dover Publications, Inc., New York

Foreword

In presenting this new work on magic, I have followed the treatment and format used in the "Magician's Manual," which gained immediate popularity when it appeared three years ago.

This new volume contains novel and up-to-date methods of magic. It combines new devices with improvements of workable tricks. All have been carefully selected and designed for efficient results.

In addition to complete descriptions and explanatory illustrations, this work also includes the most noteworthy feature established with the "Magician's Manual," namely, the actual apparatus required for certain of the tricks.

These items of apparatus are printed on inserted sheets of cardboard, ready for removal. Thus the reader is provided with the necessary equipment for his magical programs. The only other articles that he will need are either common objects or material that is easily obtainable.

Those who take this book as their guide to legerdemain will find that magic is easily performed and most entertaining not only to those who witness it, but to the performer as well. I am confident that those who study this new volume will gain the same enjoyment that was found by the readers of the "Magician's Manual," and that readers familiar with the previous work will appreciate the new repertoires that this book provides.

WALTER B. GIBSON

Published in Canada by General Publishing Company, Ltd., 30 Lesmill Road, Don Mills, Toronto, Ontario.

This Dover edition, first published in 1975, is an unabridged republication of the work originally published by David Kemp & Company, New York, in 1936.

International Standard Book Number: 0-486-23113-5
Library of Congress Catalog Card Number: 73-87046

Manufactured in the United States of America
Dover Publications, Inc.
180 Varick Street
New York, N.Y. 10014

Table of Contents

Introduction To Magic

HOW TO LEARN MAGIC Magic is easily and enjoyably learned. Unlike other accomplishments it does not require long preliminary practice. The best way to learn magic is to perform it; hence in almost his first lesson the beginner starts his career as a practicing magician. With many tricks, only a brief preliminary rehearsal is necessary.

WHERE PRACTICE IS NEEDED Practice should come *after* preliminary performances. Only by testing your tricks in public can you learn their effectiveness. Certainly to become a proficient magician, one must practice in between times. In fact some skillful feats of sleight of hand require hours of difficult training. In magic, however, the result does not depend primarily upon skill; but upon certain principles of presentation.

USE OF MISDIRECTION The vital principle of magical deception is MISDIRECTION—the art of misleading the attention of the observers. This is the real key to success. It gains results where mere deftness will not deceive. Every trick requires utilization of this one principle. Popular opinion has it that "the quickness of the hand deceives the eye." This erroneous belief serves the magician well. He knows a fact which his audience does not know, namely that quickness is merely a subterfuge.

THE AID TO MISDIRECTION Surprise is the chief aid to misdirection. This gives us a double rule to follow. Do not state beforehand just what the climax of a trick is to be; also, do not repeat the same trick at one occasion. By following these points you make it practically impossible for people to catch the trick in its early stages since they do not know what they are to expect.

CERTAIN EXCEPTIONS There are certain exceptions to the above rule. Some tricks do bear repetition; in fact should be done more than once. These, however, are tricks of a specific type, that have been designed for repetition. In some cases their effectiveness depends upon a second showing. Actually the repetition is part of the whole effect. Wherever these tricks are explained in this book they are specified as being suited for repetition.

TWO VIEW-   Magic, when presented, must be judged from two view-
POINTS OF   points. First, that of the spectator; second, that of the
MAGIC   magician. The EFFECT is the trick as the spectator sees
it. The METHOD is the trick as the magician knows it.
The beginner should study every trick from these two
standpoints. He will not find it difficult; on the contrary
he will realize that magic is rendered easy when he keeps
this double idea in mind.

THE BEST   The simplest tricks are the best. You will appreciate this
TRICKS   more and more as you do magic. You will find that when
complicated methods are eliminated, you can devote full
attention to the trick itself. This is a reason why you should
keep your methods to yourself. Many people think that
because they know how a trick is done, they have the real
secret. Such is not the case. To know a trick, you must be
able to do it.

METHOD OF   The method of instruction used in this volume is fitted to
INSTRUCTION   the principles of magic as outlined. The tricks have been
carefully chosen, not only for their merit but because they
are easily learned and can be presented with a minimum of
practice. With each trick the Effect is first described and
the Method follows. Special attention is also given to points
of presentation.

SPECIAL   Certain tricks are dependent upon special appliances rather
APPLIANCES   than upon ordinary objects. Tricks with apparatus have
been included in this volume; and the needed equipment
is supplied on special cardboard inserts, ready to be cut
out and put to immediate use.

MAGICAL   Since this volume is divided into sections covering various
PROGRAMS   types of informal magic, programs of different sorts may
be formed. A special section has been devoted to such
arrangements, carrying charts that will serve the reader
as an effective guide.

ADDITION-   In order that programs may be elaborated so that the stu-
AL MAGIC   dent may vary his repertoire, an additional section has been
included. This contains extra tricks of various types. Once
familiar with the tricks explained in the instruction pages,
the study of these added methods will become a simple
matter. Thus optional methods and diversified effects may
be acquired.

IMPROMPTU MAGIC

The tricks in this section are suited for close range performance. They can be learned with very little practice; and wherever special items are required, the needed objects are provided.

The entire show can be carried in your pocket, yet it will provide a half hour of baffling entertainment. All points of proper presentation are covered in the instructions.

Choose your own program from among these tricks; rehearse it a few times and you will be ready to give your performance under almost any conditions. The tricks themselves are designed to conceal the secret methods upon which they depend.

TRICKS IN THIS SECTION

Find the Matches

Ordinary match boxes are the items used in this trick; but extraordinary results are accomplished with them. Hence the trick will prove to be an excellent one for all impromptu performances.

THE EFFECT

The magician shows three match boxes; two are empty, one is filled with matches. He shakes the full box; the matches rattle. He moves the match boxes about the table; shakes one empty one and then the other. People are asked to pick the full match box, which they do.

Repeating the procedure, the magician leaves two match boxes on the table and drops the third in his pocket. Again, the tell-tale rattle has enabled the spectators to pick the full box. It is the one that went into the magician's pocket.

Bringing out the full box, the magician repeats the movement of the boxes. This time, the spectators pick the wrong box. They think that an empty one is the full one. Time and again, the magician baffles them. Always, the full box shows up at an unexpected spot.

THE METHOD

Four match boxes are used. At the beginning, you have three on the table: a full box and two empties. In your pocket you have another full box; but it differs slightly from the one on the table.

The box in your pocket must be so fully packed with matches that none of them will rattle. Opened, it shows as a full box of matches. Closed, it will make no noise when you shake it.

When this extra box is used in place of the first full one, people think it is empty when you shake it. By shaking it along with one empty box, you naturally make persons suppose that the third box—which you do not shake—is the full one.

Thus when you open the supposedly full box, it is empty, while a box presumed empty turns out to be filled with matches. The reason that you start with a loosely packed full box is so that a rattle will be heard at the outset. After you exchange one full box for the other, you can fool the audience every time.

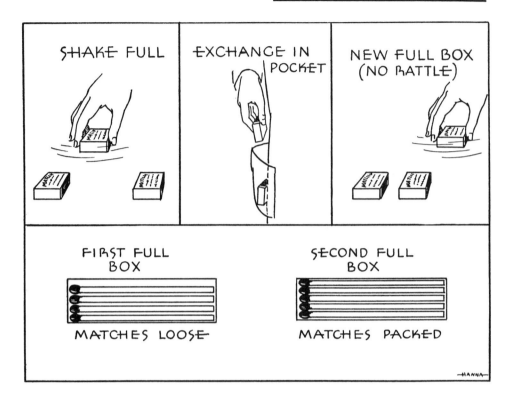

SHAKE FULL   EXCHANGE IN POCKET   NEW FULL BOX (NO RATTLE)

FIRST FULL BOX   SECOND FULL BOX

MATCHES LOOSE   MATCHES PACKED

—HANNA—

PRESENTATION

The important thing in this trick is a routine that will enable you to make a natural exchange of one full box for the other. The following procedure shows how this can be accomplished.

Start with the full box that rattles. Shake it and mix it about with the empties. Shake one empty; then the other. Mix the match boxes somewhat gingerly, using both hands to lift one over the other and push them to new positions on the table.

Ask the spectators to pick the full box; they do so, without difficulty. You open the full box, show the matches and shake it when you close it. Mix the match boxes more rapidly this time, shaking one empty; then the other. Quickly carry the full box to your pocket.

Ask where the full box is. People say: "In your pocket." Dropping the box in your pocket, you bring out the other full box, which is tightly packed. Open it and show it full of matches. Close it and place it with the empties.

This time, you *do not* shake the full box until after you have quickly mixed the boxes on the table. The spectators lose trace of the full one. Pick up an empty; shake it violently. Pick up the full box and shake it just as hard. The packed matches prevent it from rattling. The spectators think that the third, unshaken box must be the full one.

Mix the boxes gingerly, but at fair speed, as though trying to prevent a rattle. Spectators follow the box that you did not shake. They call it the full one. Open that box and show it empty. Show the full box elsewhere.

Repeat this routine, never shaking the full box while the spectators know which one it is. After you have fooled them three or four times, dump the matches from the full box to show that it is an ordinary one.

When you replace the matches in the box, leave some on the table, for use in another trick. When you pocket the nearly full match box, give it an "accidental" shake, so that it will rattle.

COMMENT

While this trick can be worked with only three match boxes, two empties and one packed full, the use of the original loosely-packed box is a subtle feature. It allows the spectators to *hear* a rattle at the beginning of the trick, which is better than having them take a rattle for granted.

No one will suspect the exchange of the full match boxes as it occurs before you begin to fool the observers. Since you put a full box in your pocket and bring a full one out, there is no cause for suspicion.

The Balanced Handkerchief

A neat impromptu trick, suitable for close-range performance. Note the two methods used in the complete effect.

THE EFFECT

The magician shows a freshly-ironed handkerchief and
spreads it on the table. Taking the center, he lifts it. The handkerchief stands upright on the table.

Removing the handkerchief, the magician shows that there
is nothing beneath it. He spreads the handkerchief upon his left
hand; lifts the center with his right. This time, the handkerchief balances upon the hand.

THE METHOD

The first part of the trick is designed to divert suspicion
from the second stage. Similarly, the second balance offsets any
doubt concerning the first.

The original balance is a simple matter. Merely draw up
the center of the spread-out handkerchief and it will stand like

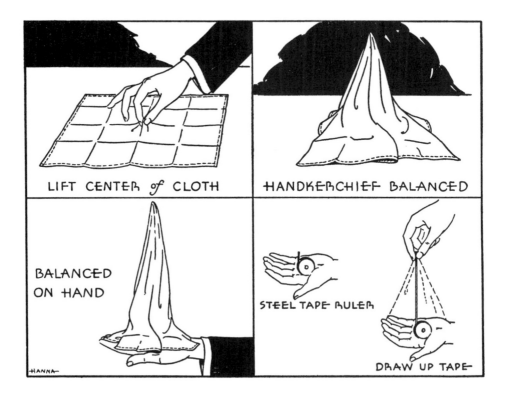

LIFT CENTER of CLOTH   HANDKERCHIEF BALANCED

BALANCED
ON HAND

STEEL TAPE RULER

DRAW UP TAPE

a miniature pyramid, the pleats aiding in its support. After the balance, lift the handkerchief; call attention to the fact that there was nothing beneath it.

Do this with your right hand. In your left, you have a cylindrical ruler of the slide-out type. It is out of sight, for the back of your hand is toward the spectators. Drape the handkerchief over the left hand. Turn the left hand palm upward. Through the cloth, grip the end of the metal tape and draw it upward.

Simply steady the cylinder with thumb and fingers. It will stay in position while the stiff tape balances the handkerchief. Finally, push the center of the handkerchief downward with the right hand. Pocket the handkerchief with your left and let the metal cylinder drop in your pocket.

PRESENTATION

No set patter is necessary for the trick. Simply demonstrate the table version first, with comment that you intend to balance the handkerchief. Have the cylinder in your left hand.

When you lift the handkerchief, flick it toward the table, to show that there is nothing on the table. As spectators look toward the table, announce that you will repeat the balance; at the same time, drape the cloth over the left hand.

By being very deliberate in the first stage of the trick, as though the feat presented great difficulty, you can take your time with the second balance. Thus you will have no trouble finding the tip of the sliding tape.

Stiff-taped rulers are easily obtained. The smaller the size, the better, as you need only a short length of tape. After you have pocketed the handkerchief, you can remove it a few moments later, under pretext of using it in another trick. The cylindrical ruler remains in your pocket.

The Rising Cigarette

This is an improvement over an older trick. In its present form, it is one of the handiest and best of impromptu feats in magic.

THE EFFECT

The magician takes an opened pack of cigarettes from his pocket. He holds the pack in one hand; makes passes above it with the other hand. A cigarette rises from the pack. The cigarettes and the pack are quite unprepared; they may be handled freely later.

THE METHOD

Use a pack of twenty cigarettes that is wrapped in cellophane. Open the pack at the top, tearing away a portion of the paper; but leave the cellophane wrapper around the pack.

Take out some of the cigarettes—about half of them—and insert one of the cigarettes between the outside of the pack and the cellophane. The insertion should be made at the back of the pack.

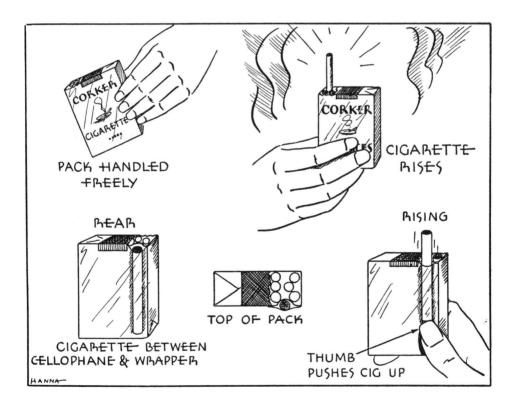

PACK HANDLED FREELY

CIGARETTE RISES

REAR

RISING

CIGARETTE BETWEEN CELLOPHANE & WRAPPER

TOP OF PACK

THUMB PUSHES CIG UP

HANNA

You may then carry this pack in your pocket like any pack of cigarettes. When you bring it from your pocket, you can take one or two cigarettes from it in ordinary fashion; but always keep the extra cigarette away from the audience.

Hold the pack in your left hand, fingers at the front and thumb at the back. Keep the pack upright, with the front toward the spectators. Make passes with your right hand; at the same time push the left thumb against the cellophane *below* the outside cigarette.

Raising the thumb forces the cigarette into view. It rises and seemingly comes from within the pack. When the cigarette is almost from the pack, remove it the rest of the distance with the right hand.

PRESENTATION

The trick should be presented in a rather casual fashion. You may bring out the pack and work the trick immediately if you wish; but if you have occasion to do so, it is preferable to first remove a few cigarettes in the ordinary manner.

Call attention to the pack as you hold it. Wait until attention is properly centered before you start the rising cigarette. Make the action slow and steady; the cigarette will come up straight and with smooth motion.

It is best to have the pack torn open at the side to your right; and to have the cigarette placed behind that spot. Thus the left thumb can come across in back of the pack and be entirely hidden during its action.

If the top is roughly torn and the pack pressed somewhat flat, the illusion will be perfect at the closest range. The trick should be practiced in front of a mirror in order to perfect it; for although the method is simple, with no skill required, it can be made smoother through rehearsal.

The Changing Match Pack

This is a neat trick when presented in impromptu fashion. It forms an excellent stunt when introduced into a series of other tricks.

THE EFFECT

The magician brings a pack of paper matches from his pocket. He shows it from both sides, calling attention to the red printing on its cover. Holding the closed match pack in his left hand, he passes his right in front of it.

Immediately, the match pack changes both design and color. Its printing is different; it is green instead of red. The magician shows it back and front; again passes his hand over it. The match pack returns to its original appearance.

THE METHOD

A special match pack is used. It is simply a strip of cardboard, printed on both sides; but one side is red, the other green.

A length of striking surface should be removed from an ordinary match pack and pasted to the bottom of the cardboard

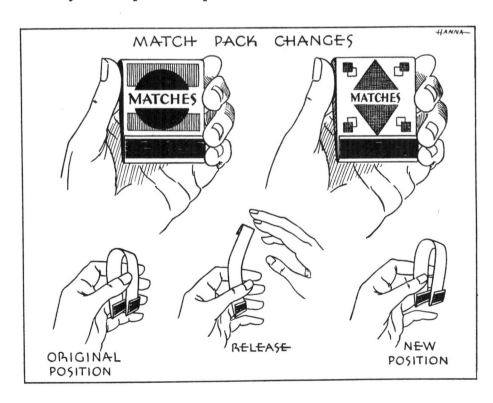

MATCH PACK CHANGES

MATCHES   MATCHES

ORIGINAL POSITION   RELEASE   NEW POSITION

strip. Similarly, a second piece of striking surface should be pasted to the bottom of the other side.

The *bottom* of one side is the *top* of the other. The different designs are simply inverted, as printed.

Since this is an imitation match pack, the proper way to show it is with the flap bent backward. It will then give a perfect appearance of a *closed* match pack. To exhibit it properly, hold the fake pack between the thumb and first fingers of the left hand. Keep the thumb stretched up one side of the pack; the fingers at the other side. From this position, it is a simple matter to show both sides of the supposed pack, by a turn of the hand.

Bring the right hand over and in front of the match pack. Release the bent-back flap. It will spring forward. The right hand draws it down, frontward. The left fingers and thumb regain their grip. When the right hand moves away, the match pack is seen in its new condition. It has simply been turned inside out.

Both sides of the folded pack may be shown as before. Another covering by the right hand enables you to change the pack back to its original condition. After a few changes, simply drop the pack in the left coat pocket.

PRESENTATION

This is a quick type of trick and should be presented briskly. Simply show the pack; remark upon its design and the color of its printing. Tell people to watch it closely and witness the result.

Pass the right hand over the pack; extend it close to the eyes of the observers. Call attention to the fact that the design is different and that the color is green. Repeat the stunt in the same fashion and finally pocket the pack without comment.

After that proceed with another trick.

The special strip necessary for this trick is printed on one of the cardboard inserts in this volume. It may be cut out and prepared in the manner described. With it are printed two ordinary match pack covers; one for each of the special designs. These can be prepared like ordinary match packs, with matches in them.

Some time after the trick has been shown, you may find occasion to produce one of the ordinary packs and take a match from it. Make no comment about it when you do so; simply let persons observe the pack closely enough to see that it is ordinary.

The Chinaman's Head

In itself, this trick is a brief one. The story that goes with it is the feature that heightens the effect and aids in the deception. Therefore, the presentation should be studied and rehearsed as an essential portion of the trick.

THE EFFECT

The magician states that he will demonstrate a novel means of execution used in China, chopping off a head with a rope. He uses a wooden match to represent the Chinaman. Lighting the match, the magician burns the head, then blows out the flame. He holds the match with the head upward.

From his own head, the magician takes a hair and winds it about the neck of the miniature Chinaman. He gives the hair a sharp tug. Instantly, the head pops from the match.

THE METHOD

The match is burned with the head held upward so that only a short stretch of burned wood supports the match head.

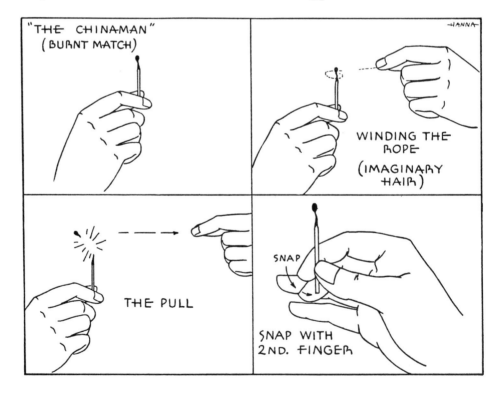

"THE CHINAMAN" (BURNT MATCH)

—HANNA

WINDING THE ROPE

(IMAGINARY HAIR)

THE PULL

SNAP

SNAP WITH 2ND. FINGER

The match is held between the thumb and forefinger of the right hand in an upright position.

Allow about a quarter inch of the match to project below the right forefinger. Have the second finger pressed against that lower tip. The left hand then pretends to take a hair and wind it around the bottom of the match head.

The left hand makes a quick tug to the left, as though pulling the imaginary hair. As you jerk the left hand, snap your right second finger inward. The leverage against the lower end of the match will cause the match head to pop off. The sudden motion of the left hand draws attention from the quick snap of the right second finger.

PRESENTATION

(Paragraphs in *italics* are references to steps described under presentation.)

The presentation of this trick is dependent upon the story that accompanies it. Use the following patter, subject to any variations which you choose to make. Note, however, how certain portions of the talk are suited to the action.

"In China, it is customary to execute certain criminals—particularly pirates—by beheading them. The authorities in the European sections of the Chinese cities prefer to hang such criminals. A conflict of the authorities happened to cause trouble for a Chinese executioner.

"A pirate had been sentenced to death; and the executioner was told to hang him in the European fashion. He knew that the Chinese would make trouble unless the pirate was beheaded, so the executioner rigged up an invention of his own. I shall demonstrate exactly how he handled it.

"This match represents the Chinese pirate." *Hold match upright in right hand.* "We need something to represent a rope. Ah! A hair will be just the thing." *Pretend to pluck a hair from your head.* "Yes, this hair is just about the right length. The executioner wound the rope three times around the Chinaman's neck." *Pretend to wind the hair around the match.* "He drew the rope tight." *Pretend to tighten the hair.* "All was ready."

Pause as though waiting for a signal.

"The signal was given. One—two—pull!" *Pretend to tug the hair.* "Away went the Chinaman's head and everybody was happy." *Pretend to drop the hair on the floor; then add:* "Everybody except the dead Chinaman."

Toss the match on the table as a finish.

Spot the Spot

This is an improvement on an earlier trick with spotted cards. In its present form the spot trick requires only two cards which change position although they never leave the sight of the spectators.

THE EFFECT

Two cards are shown. One is adorned with a large green spot; the other has a red spot of about the same size. The magician asks the spectators which they prefer: red or green.

A choice being made, he turns the cards toward himself and moves them from hand to hand. Finally, he slides one card directly in back of the other. He draws that card away with his right hand. He turns the spotted side toward the spectators and they see the green spot.

As he starts to place the green spot card in his pocket, the magician stops. Instead, he gives the card to a spectator, to hold spot downward. Retaining the red spot card, the magician orders a magical transposition.

Immediately, he turns his card toward the audience to show that its spot is GREEN. The spectator, holding what he thinks is the green spot card, looks at it to find that its spot is RED.

THE METHOD

In addition to the two spotted cards, you have a loose green spot, slightly larger than the one printed on the green spot card. When you first show the spot cards, have this loose spot OVER the green spot on the printed card. You must hold it in position with your thumb; hence it is necessary to handle the green spot card with care. The other card with the red spot can be freely handled.

Holding a card in each hand, turn them toward yourself and slide them together a few times, shifting them from hand to hand. All the while, be careful to keep the loose green spot out of sight. This is easy as it no longer has to be kept in a central position.

When the spectators are no longer sure which card is which, slide the red-spotted card between the loose green spot and the green-spotted card. With your thumbs, adjust the loose green spot over the red spot.

This card is the one that you take away in your right hand no matter which color is chosen. Keep the green spot over the red; turn the spotted side of the card so that the spectators can see it; then turn the card toward yourself and start to place the card in your coat pocket.

There, you pause. Up to this point you have kept the loose spot in position with your thumb. Simply release the loose spot; let it drop into your pocket under cover of the card. The card has nothing but a printed red spot; so you give it—spot downward—to a spectator.

Naturally, he thinks that he has the green spot card; that the card in your left hand is red-spotted. In mysterious fashion, you command the cards to change places. The spectator finds that he has the RED card; you have the GREEN. To add to the surprise, you immediately give your green spot card for examination along with the red spotter.

PRESENTATION

Start this trick in casual fashion; lay emphasis upon the choice of color, because it is unimportant. At the finish, stress the mystery about to be accomplished. After the spots have been transposed, you can show hesitation in giving the green spot card for examination. That will draw attention from the fact that the trick was really done with the red spot card.

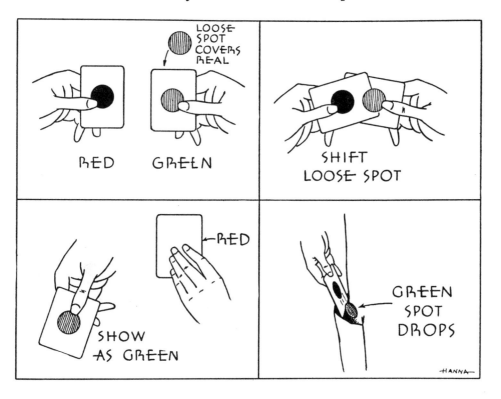

The following patter brings out these points of presentation.

"Here is a simple experiment in psychology. I use two cards with colored spots, because they are so conspicuous that they may be easily remembered. I turn the spots away from you and move the cards about a bit.

"Let us see how good your memories are. What were the colors of the spots? Red and green you say. Very good. Will some one pick one of those two colors? You say green? I shall take the green spot and place it in my pocket. Here it is. Wait! You chose it; therefore I shall ask you to hold it with the spot downward.

"Of course you remember your own color. Green. But green is a magic color. So magical, that it can vanish. Of course it must go somewhere, so I shall call it here. Look, I have the green card. Yours has a red spot? Of course! I sent you the red in place of the green."

If the spectator chooses red instead of green, simply change the patter.

"You choose red? Very well; we no longer need the green card. I shall place it in my pocket. No, wait; perhaps you had better hold it. We shall keep the green spot turned down, so it will not disturb us.

"I hold the red card that you chose. Watch this amazing result. One—two—go!" Flip the card. "The red spot has vanished. Look! I have the green spot instead. You have the red spot on your card? Certainly. You asked for it, so you have it."

The cards necessary for this trick, together with the special spot required, will be found, ready to be cut out, upon one of the cardboard inserts in this volume.

Metal Through Metal

The simplicity of the objects required in this trick make it an excellent impromptu stunt. Though more of a puzzle than a mystery, its novelty will always intrigue those who witness it.

THE EFFECT

Two safety pins are locked together. The magician takes the safety pins; clicks them one way, then another, to show that they are firmly fastened. Suddenly, he draws the safety pins apart; hands them immediately to the spectators. The pins are separated; yet each one is clamped as firmly as before.

THE METHOD

The trick is simply to pull the safety pins so that the bar of one, slides between the point and clasp of the other, so neatly that the second pin snaps back to closed position. To do this, you must know the exact way in which to hold the pins.

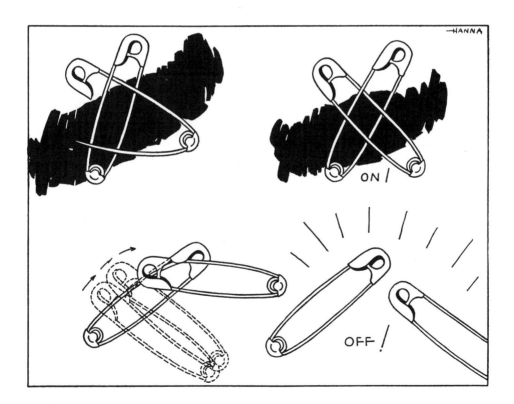

The pins are locked with their loose bars to the left. The loose bar of the right hand pin goes above that of the left hand pin, as illustrated in the upper diagrams. The pins are held by the small ends. Draw the hands apart; the pins will come loose, but will remain closed.

There is also another way of locking the pins, which can be used as a variation. It is not illustrated; but with the pins at hand, the following explanation will suffice:

Close one safety pin. Hold it by the small end. Keep it level, with the clasp *away* from you and the loose bar to the *right*. Push the point of the other pin straight up, just to the *left* of the loose bar of the first pin. Clasp the second pin.

Swing the second pin so its solid bar is toward you, and lay it downward to the left, so it is almost flat upon the first pin. The clasp of the second pin is toward your left. Take the clasp of the second pin between your right thumb and forefinger, the thumb above.

While the left thumb and forefinger firmly hold the small end of the first pin, slide your right hand forward and to the right. It pulls the second pin by the clasp. The solid bar of the second pin comes under the clasp of the first pin and the second pin slides free. The first pin will clasp again.

PRESENTATION

Merely call attention to the safety pins; lock them together and show one hanging from the other. Pull them a few times, to bluff the spectators; then place the pins in the required position.

Draw the pins apart smoothly, with a rather smart pull; but do not jerk them, nor make the move too slowly. A neat sliding motion will separate them so quickly that the eye can not detect the passage.

Be sure to use fairly large safety pins that are in good condition. When you have the knack no one can possibly see any motion of the bars at the time of separation. The point of the first pin does not come far enough inward to be observed.

Always place the pins in the hands of the spectators so that they can see that the safety pins are still clamped. It is safe to repeat this trick a few times; but always fake a few false moves before putting the pins in their proper position.

Odds and Evens

This is an impromptu trick with coins, wherein three spectators assist the magician. Coins may be borrowed for the trick; but as a large number of pennies are required, it is advisable to have your own supply before you begin.

THE EFFECT

The magician shows a quantity of coins. He tells three spectators that he will present a problem in odds and evens. First, the magician takes some of the coins for himself.

He then tells one person (designated as A) to pick up any number of coins he chooses; but to take pennies only from the table. Since there are considerably more than ten pennies on the table, this allows a wide choice.

The person is told to count his coins; to remember whether his total is ODD or EVEN. This is done while the magician's back is turned.

A second person, B, is told to pick up all the coins that remain on the table. He holds them concealed in his hand like A. He does not have to count them.

The magician has some coins of his own. He gives these to the third person C, and tells him to hold them in his hand without counting them at all.

From his pocket, the magician brings some additional pennies. He turns to A and says:

"You hold a number of pennies. You know whether the amount is ODD or EVEN, but I do not. Whichever you have, odd or even, I am going to make it the opposite. Here: take these pennies along with your own."

A adds the extra coins to his own. The magician states: "Remember, I have changed the amount from odd to even; or from even to odd. Which did you have to begin with?"

If A replies: "An odd number," the magician states: "You have an even number." If A answers: "An even number," the magician says: "You have an odd number."

In both cases, the magician adds: "Remember my statement; but do not count the coins until afterward."

Ignoring B for the moment, the magician turns to C and says: "I gave you some coins myself. I know whether the total is odd or even; but you do not. I am going to have YOU name either odd or even. You yourself will tell which amount you hold, even though you have not counted the coins. Name your choice."

C says "odd" or "even" as he chooses. The magician tells him to hold his coins.

Turning to B, the magician states: "In your case, I shall tell you whether your coins are odd or even, although I do not know how many coins you took." The magician then states "odd" or "even."

A counts out his pennies. They prove to be odd or even, according to which the magician says. B counts his coins. They are odd or even according to the magician's statement. C counts his coins; for the first time, he learns their total. His coins are ODD or EVEN according to his OWN statement!

THE METHOD

This trick depends upon a variety of principles; hence it is difficult to detect. Nevertheless, the procedure is simple and the trick practically works itself. The routine, however, must be carefully followed.

First: after the coins are placed upon the table, gather up some for yourself. See to it that there are dimes and nickels on the table, along with a large number of pennies.

Pick up *all* of the dimes, a few of the nickels, and some of the pennies. Leave an EVEN number of coins on the table, in pennies and nickels.

Tell A to take some pennies; to note whether they are odd or even. Tell B to gather all the coins that remain. Meanwhile, your back is turned. From the coins that you hold, count off a dime, two nickels and four pennies. When A and B have their coins, place your coins in C's hand. Tell him to hold them without counting them.

From your pocket, produce an ODD number of pennies. Five is about the right number. Give them to A, without letting him count them. Tell him: "If your total was ODD, it will now be EVEN. If it was EVEN, it will now be ODD."

Ask him which the total WAS and remind him that it will be the opposite. This always happens when you add an odd number to odd or even. So you are safe with A.

From A, however, you learn a fact that you want. Whatever his total was—ODD or EVEN—B's total will be the same. That was because you started with an even number of coins on the table. Thus you KNOW B's total, from the standpoint of odd or even. To cover that fact, you ignore B and speak to C.

Let C choose ODD or EVEN for himself. You are sure to have it right, for you gave him SEVEN coins (an odd number) that totalled 24 CENTS (an even amount). You then turn to B and tell him that his coins are ODD or EVEN, according to the fact that you learned from A.

Have A count his coins first. They come out odd or even as you predicted. Ask B to give you his coins, so that you can count them. You do; and they prove ODD or EVEN just as you told B they were. However, when you count B's coins, you must remember C.

If C chose ODD, simply count B's coins one by one. If C chose EVEN, count B's coins according to AMOUNT. B has some nickels, so you count them as five each; then count the pennies as one each. Do this aloud. In either case, the total will be the same from the standpoint of odd or even.

Coming to C, you naturally count in the same fashion as you did with B. If you counted B's coins as one apiece, you do the same with C's, thus finding a total of SEVEN, for an odd number. If you counted B's coins according to their values, you do the same with C's and end with 24 cents, an even total.

COMMENT

You can allow an odd number of coins on the table, if you wish. In that case, if A declares that his total WAS odd, you will know that B's total IS even. If A says that his total WAS even, you will know that B's total IS odd.

You can also use quarters instead of nickels if you choose; or half dollars instead of dimes. But be sure that pennies are plentiful and that you have the odd number of extra pennies in your pocket. Also that no dimes or half dollars are on the table.

Always have A count his coins first, when you reach the finale of the trick. Since he has pennies only, the number of coins will equal the amount. Count B's yourself, right after A's, so that you can count for number of coins or for amount, in preparation for C.

The trick may be performed with foreign coins. Those that are based on the decimal system can be handled in the same fashion as United States coins. In the case of English money, use English pennies instead of cents; three-penny pieces instead of five cent nickels; and sixpenny pieces (or shillings) in place of the ten cent dimes.

The Jail Escape

Colored cards are the participants in this mystery. While the trick appears to require skill, you will find that the cards themselves take care of the result.

THE EFFECT

The magician shows an empty hat, which represents a theater. He picks up a small card and shows it on both sides. The card is entirely red. It represents an escape artist, who has promised to release himself from the local jail.

The magician drops the red card in the hat. He shows three green cards, held in a fan, exhibiting them on both sides. These are rookie policemen. He places the three green cards in the hat.

Two of the policemen take the escape king to jail. To demonstrate this, the magician removes two green cards from the hat, with the red card between them. He puts them in his coat pocket which serves as the prison cell and brings out the two green policemen.

Thus the escape artist is in prison (the magician's pocket), while one of the policemen has remained in the theater (otherwise the hat).

Then comes the finish. Reaching in his pocket, the magician brings out the card that he placed there. It is GREEN. By mistake, the two policemen have jailed their own pal!

Reaching into the hat, the magician produces the RED card. The escape king has slipped one over on the law. He is back in his dressing room at the theater!

THE METHOD

Five cards are used in the trick. There are three green cards and one red one. There is also a special card, half red and half green. Each side is divided diagonally, to form the two colors; but the diagonal lines are opposite on front and back. That is an important feature of the special card.

To begin the trick, you previously place one green card in your coat pocket. Arrange the two other green cards with the special card, so that the three form a fan. The special card must be between the greens, fixed so that only its green half shows.

You hold these three cards in your right hand. The hat and the red card are on the table. Show the hat empty, with your left hand. Pick up the red card with your left, and drop the red card in the hat.

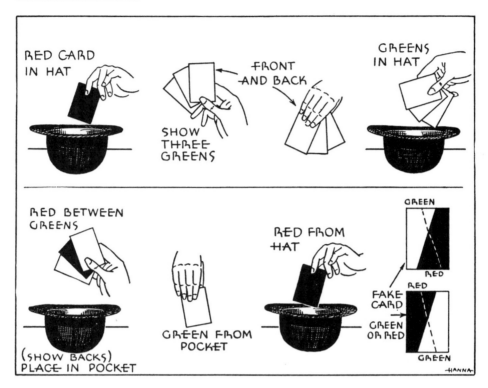

Show the three cards in your right hand, exhibiting them as three greens and calling them such. Turn them over so that the spectators can see the backs. The opposite diagonals make the cards appear as three greens, no matter which side is shown. Drop the fanned cards into the hat.

Reaching into the hat, you turn the special card around and arrange it between the two greens so that when you bring them out fanned, there is a red card showing between two greens. Exhibit both sides of the fan. Place the three cards in your coat pocket.

There, you release the special card and bring out the two green ones. Lay them on the table. Reach in your pocket and bring out the extra green card, leaving the special card in your pocket.

For the finish, you bring the red card from the hat.

Note: If you are careful when you place the three cards in the pocket, you can tell whether the special card goes outside the extra green one, or inside of it. That known, you can bring out the extra green without hesitation. If you are not sure, glance into your pocket from above, when you reach for the extra green card. You can then pick the card correctly when you draw it from your pocket.

PRESENTATION

It is the presentation which enables you to perform this trick to best advantage. Stand in back of the table where you have placed the hat. Always face the table except when calling direct attention to the fanned cards in your right hand. Then turn slightly to the right.

When you place the fanned cards in your pocket, however, you should face the spectators and retain that position for the remainder of the trick. Synchronize your actions with the following patter, which tells the story and should therefore serve as the outline of your talk.

"You have probably heard of Houdini and the other escape kings who used to be locked in jail cells, only to escape. People still wonder how they did it. I shall explain the system.

"The stunt always began at the theater, where the escape king made his headquarters. So we shall let this hat represent the theater. The theater is empty, because the stunt always took place in the morning.

"This red card is the escape king. He enters the theater and waits there for the police. Here are the officers; three green cops; for the police chief always sends rookies who have no regular beat. They enter the theater: there, two of them handcuff the escape king between them. That takes only a few moments. When the two cops come out, they have the escape king properly secured.

"They leave the third policeman at the theater to call up the police chief." *Hold three cards fanned with right hand; point to hat with left.* "Then the two cops take the escape king to the jail and chuck him in a dark cell. My pocket will be the jail cell.

"After they manage to unclip the handcuffs, the cops come out. They stand on guard and wait for the police chief." *Separate the two green cards. Show one in each hand, back and front.* "The police chief arrives; they tell him that the escape king is in the cell."

At this point, place the two green cards on the table. Show the hands empty and resume.

"The police chief unlocks the cell and orders the escape king to come out. The occupant of the cell comes out. But he is NOT the escape king. To his astonishment, the police chief sees the rookie cop who called him on the telephone, from the theater!"

Show the extra green card, both sides, with the right hand. Transfer it to the left.

"So the police chief hops over to the theater. When he gets there, who does he find? Who else but the escape king, back in his dressing room, calling up the newspapers to tell them how he bluffed the police chief."

Reach in the hat with the right hand. Bring out the red card. Show it on both sides. Transfer it to the left hand, with the green card that you hold there. Pick up the hat with the right hand. Show it empty.

"The theater, you see, is still empty. But it will be packed for the matinee. So now you should know how it was done. If you are not quite sure, you are free to interview the escape king and the three rookie cops."

Pass the red card and the three greens for examination.

"Maybe they will tell you more about it. But don't ask ME any questions. I am only the police chief. I didn't arrive until after it was all over, so I know nothing."

The five special cards needed for this trick are printed upon one of the inserted cardboard sheets contained in this volume. Cut out the cards and they will serve as the necessary apparatus.

Eleven Cents

A puzzling impromptu stunt can often be made into an excellent trick by proper presentation. Such is the case with this one. While you offer to show a stunt that "any one can do," people find themselves unable to accomplish it even after they have seen it done.

THE EFFECT

Five coins are laid on the table; three pennies and two dimes; they are arranged in alternating order, so that no two coins of the same denomination come side by side.

The problem is to move the coins two at a time, to new positions. Each move must be made with two coins that are side by side, and eleven cents must be shifted with each move. That is, a penny and a dime must figure in each action. At the end of four moves, pennies and dimes are to form separate groups.

The performer accomplishes this swiftly and smoothly, with four simple moves. It looks easy; but when spectators attempt the trick, they bungle. Even when the moves are repeated, they fail to catch the system.

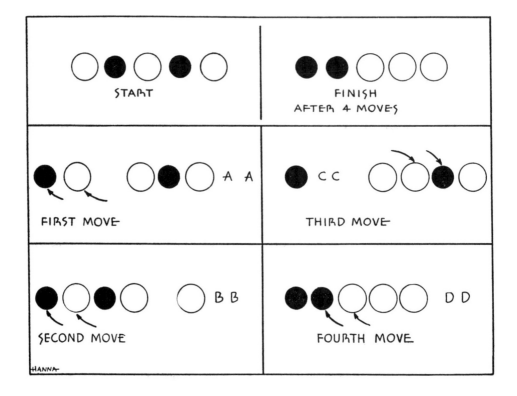

THE METHOD

The moves follow a definite rule. On every move except the third, have a dime on the *left* of the pair you move. On the third move, a *penny* must be on the left. Certain moves are obvious if you follow this system; but there are other points to be remembered. Practice the moves as follows.

First Move: Move either dime and the penny to the right of it. Slide the pair to the left end of the line, but leave a space of about two inches between that pair and the penny which marks the original left end of the line.

Second Move: Move the other dime and the penny to the right of it; carry them to the left of the first pair.

Third Move: Only one dime has a penny to the left of it. Move that dime and the penny on its left. Carry them *between* the two remaining pennies.

Fourth Move: Take the dime and penny which are on the right end of the line. Move them in between the other dime and two pennies.

The final arrangement is thus obtained. The coins are segregated; two dimes at the left, three pennies at the right.

COMMENT

In moving the coin, place the forefinger on one and the second finger on the other. This enables swift action as you slide the pair along the table. As soon as one move is completed, shift to another pair and make an immediate move.

It is important to allow a space between the pair first moved, and the penny, which is originally the first coin at the left of the line. That space is to be used later, with the third move. It is a point that most persons neglect when they try to duplicate the trick.

Note that when the dime is on the *left;* namely in Moves One, Two and Four, the *direction* of the moves is to the *left* also. When a dime is on the *right,* in Move Three, the *direction* of the move is to the *right.* These points make it easy to remember the routine.

Moves One and Two allow the option of the only two possible pairs that fill requirements. Move Three has only one pair of coins that can be used in accordance with the rule. The same is true of Move Four.

However, the coins allow a great variety of moves that are *not* in accordance with the correct method and those are the ones that other people generally choose.

The trick can be varied with coins of other values than cents and dimes; but always use three of one type and two of another.

TABLE MAGIC

Dinner table tricks are always popular and the impromptu magician is constantly called upon to perform them. The tricks in this section are all of that type. Utilizing common objects, easily obtained, they may be presented at the dinner table, or the card table.

The tricks in this section may be easily arranged into program form so that your repertoire is by no means limited. Every trick is effective, no matter how close the onlookers may be.

In fact, some of the tricks are better at the closest possible range, and most of them require the cooperation of the spectators. You will find that all of your audiences will be impressed by these feats of close-up wizardry.

TRICKS IN THIS SECTION

The Magnetic Knife

This trick is particularly suited to the dinner table as it is performed with a table knife. If presented elsewhere, when a table knife is not available, a similar object may be used. The trick will work well with a large pencil or a ruler.

THE EFFECT

Holding a table knife in his hands, the magician folds his fingers and extends their backs toward the spectators. The table knife rests between the palms of his hands; his thumbs hold it in position.

The hands are raised to the vertical; they are clasped across in front of the magician's body. The knife is upright; part of it projects above the hands, part below. The magician announces that the knife is magnetized.

People ridicule this theory, because the magician's thumbs are out of sight and could obviously be holding the knife in its position. The magician volunteers to show his thumbs; he raises one, lowers it. He repeats the manoeuver with the other thumb. The spectators laugh, because they think that the magician is merely transferring the burden from one thumb to the other.

The laugh ends when the magician raises both thumbs. The knife does not fall. It remains behind his fingers, invisibly supported. It stays there until he pulls his hands apart; then the knife drops to the table and is immediately given for examination.

METHOD AND PRESENTATION

This trick is easily accomplished; and its secret is quite elusive. It depends upon the middle finger of the right hand. When you fold your hands, you do not do so in the ordinary fashion. Instead, you slide your fingers together, end to end.

The knife should be lying on the left palm. As you bring the right hand toward the left, bend the right second finger inward. Slide the right forefinger between the first and second fingers of the left hand. The third finger of the right hand goes between the second and third of the left. The little finger of the right hand goes between the third and little finger of the left.

When you raise the backs of the hands toward the spectators, they see only *seven* fingers instead of eight. The position of the fingers is so natural that they never think of counting the fingers. They are more interested in your thumbs, which are out of sight in the palms of your hands.

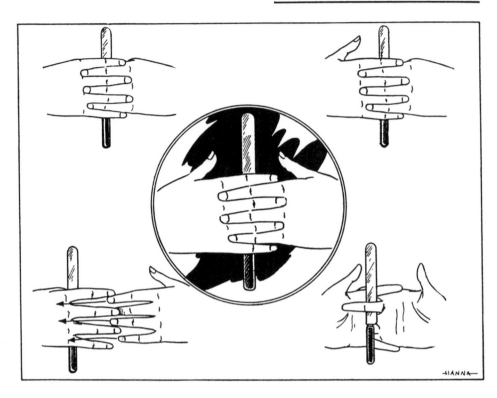

The middle finger of your right hand is on the inner side of the knife. Its pressure actually holds the knife in place. The thumbs merely appear to hold the knife. After you have kept up the bluff for a while, extend the thumb straight upward. The knife will still adhere, thanks to the support of the hidden finger.

Retain this final position just long enough to convince the spectators that the knife is actually adhering to the hands without support. Move the hands back and forth; toward the spectators and away from them. Do this deliberately, tilting the hands slightly, forward and backward. Ten seconds should be about the limit of this demonstration. At the end of that period, pull the hands apart and let the knife fall.

Show your hands separately. Let the spectators examine the knife. They will look for adhesive substances, and will be perplexed when they find none.

COMMENT

Practice the locking of the fingers until it becomes a natural process. You will find that your hands will soon learn to take the position automatically. The separation of the hands requires no practice.

The Tell-Tale Sugar

This is a divination trick that is particularly suited to the dinner table and cannot be shown properly elsewhere. Hence it is included in this section.

THE EFFECT

The magician places four or five lumps of sugar upon the table. He pushes them around a bit, changing their position, and invites spectators to do the same.

He states that he will turn his back; that while he is looking the other way, the spectators are to choose one lump of sugar. Someone is to pick up that lump and hold it to his forehead, then replace it on the table with the others.

After that, they may push any or all of the lumps to new positions; but they must not lift a second lump. That would make it impossible for the magician to concentrate upon the selected piece of sugar.

The magician turns his back, the lump of sugar is selected and lifted from the table, then replaced. When all is ready, the

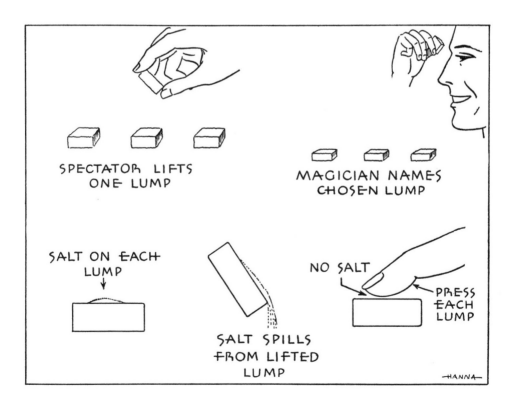

SPECTATOR LIFTS ONE LUMP

MAGICIAN NAMES CHOSEN LUMP

SALT ON EACH LUMP

SALT SPILLS FROM LIFTED LUMP

NO SALT

PRESS EACH LUMP

—HANNA—

magician turns around. He picks up each lump in turn; holds it to his forehead in order to gain the correct impression. When he comes to the chosen piece of sugar, he announces it.

METHOD AND PRESENTATION

A slight preparation is necessary; and it depends upon another dinner table material other than the lumps of sugar. The needed item is salt.

Lay the lumps of sugar near you, some time before the trick is to be performed. Upon each lump, place a small pinch of salt. The sugar is white; so is the salt. Hence the salt can not be noticed.

When you explain the purpose of the trick, you push the lumps of sugar around the table and specify that only the chosen one must be lifted. Your reason for this is that you depend upon a 'magnetic' impression. Actually, you are seeing to it that the lumps of sugar do not lose their loads of salt.

After your back is turned, some one lifts a lump of sugar. The salt falls off. Since the quantity is small, this will not be noticed. Upon the white table cloth, the grains will lie unobserved.

When the lump is replaced and pushed about with the others, you return and pick up the bits of sugar, one by one. It is not necessary to look for the salt that each lump carries. By placing your thumb on top of each lump when you lift it, you feel the salt, like a tiny cushion.

One lump will have no salt. Your thumb will sense that fact immediately. The absence of the salt tells you that the lump of sugar is the chosen one.

COMMENT

If the table is covered by a colored table-cloth, sprinkle a little salt on it beforehand and find if it shows. If the salt is not easily noticed, you can perform the trick. In this case, however, it is wise to use less salt than usual.

The Mystic Loops

There is a "catch" to this trick; one that makes it a real perplexity. You will find it more and more effective the longer it is repeated; yet no trick could be easier to learn, which makes it one of the best of all impromptu stunts.

THE EFFECT

The magician takes a piece of string and ties the ends to form a large loop about two feet in length. Crossing his hands, he draws two lengths of string to form an X inside the large loop. This produces two inner loops.

The magician asks some one to insert a finger in the loop at the left. That done, the magician pulls the right end of the string. The loops tighten and trap the spectator's finger.

Forming the loops again, the magician inserts his own finger, using his left hand. He pulls the string from the right; the loops slide away, leaving his left finger free. They seem to pass right through the finger.

Every time the trick is repeated, the result is the same. The loops are formed in the same fashion; but the spectator's finger is always trapped; the magician's invariably comes free.

THE METHOD

There are two ways of forming the loops so nearly alike that they appear to be identical. One system will trap the finger; the other will not.

Make a large loop and hold it taut between the hands; one end of the loop girding your left fingers, the other the right. Hold your palms upward.

Swing the right hand over to the left. With your right thumb and forefinger grasp the string just *below* the little finger of the left hand. Draw the right hand away, carrying the string with it.

Bring the left hand over to the right and use the left thumb and forefinger to grasp the string just *below* the little finger of the right hand. In doing this, bring the left thumb and forefinger *above* the string grasped between the right thumb and forefinger. (By "above," we mean in front of the string, in case the loops are hanging straight downward.)

Stretch the string between your hands. The loops are formed. Lay them carefully upon the table, keeping the hands palm upward as you do so. The loops are ready for the release. If you place your forefinger in the little loop at the left and draw away the outer string at the right, the loops will come clear.

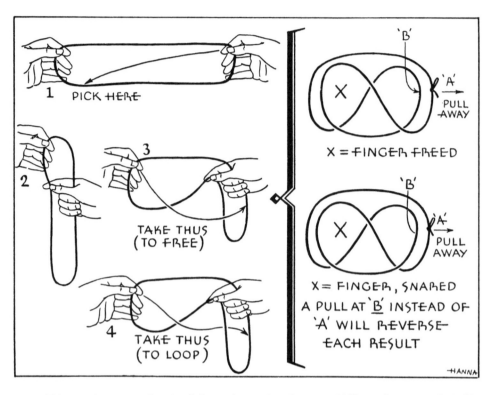

The other method of forming the loops differs in one detail. When you bring your left hand over to the right to grasp the string below the right little finger, reach *beneath* the string that is held by the right thumb and forefinger, instead of *above* it. (By "beneath," we mean in back of the string, in case the loops are hanging loose.)

Formed by this system, the loops will look exactly the same when laid upon the table; but this time, they will trap any finger that is placed in the loop at the left.

PRESENTATION

It is best first to demonstrate the trick by forming the loops to trap some one's finger. Indicate that the loops will normally be a trap. Then form loops that will release; and pull them away from your own finger.

When other persons want to try it—as they will—oblige them. Trap them every time. Intersperse these demonstrations with a few of your own releases. The trick will become more baffling with every demonstration. Yet no matter how closely the spectators watch you, they will never learn the secret, provided of course that you form the loops without hesitation.

Do not try to form the loops too rapidly. That would cause

suspicion. Draw the strings at fair speed, and practice it until you can form the loops almost automatically.

ADDITIONAL ROUTINE

One problem presents itself with this trick. If you repeat it often, some persons may wish to insert their fingers when you are about to place yours in the loop. Or, they may challenge you to insert *your own* finger after you have formed the loops for them.

Obviously, this offers complications; for you have already set the loops to trap or release. When called upon at the last moment to do the other, any excuse on your part would indicate a prearrangement of the loops.

It is wise to ignore these challenges when they are first offered, because it is never good policy to allow your audience to tell you what to do. Go ahead with your usual procedure; but if the challengers become too insistent, you can finally settle them.

Here is the method. You will notice that when you make these loops, they resemble a figure 8 on its side, within an oval. The string that you pull is the one at the extreme right, namely the string that forms the large outer loop.

If, instead of that string, you take the string that forms an end of the figure 8, the result will be exactly the opposite of your original intention. By pulling that inner string, loops set to trap will release, or loops set to catch will come free. Thus you can control matters up to the very moment that you pull the string.

No matter which set-up you have used with the loops, you can ask a spectator whether he wants to place his finger in the loop at the left, or if he wants you to insert your finger. You can guarantee to trap him, or to release your own finger.

Ordinarily, it is best to follow the usual method. When you start, have the knot of the string under your right forefinger. Then, when you pull the string away, you can do so by grasping the knot, when the loops are on the table. The knot is easy to grip and it prevents you from making any mistake.

When you find it advisable to shift to the further routine just described, start with the knot somewhere near the center of the string instead of at your right hand. Then the two strings at the right of the loops will appear exactly the same, and you can take either one you choose.

You will find that the spectators concentrate upon the loop where they put their fingers. Hence, when it is necessary to resort to the shift system, your action will not be noted provided that you pick up the proper string at the right and pull it without hesitation.

Choose Your Object

The excellence of this trick depends upon the fact that ordinary objects are used. While it is a divination trick, it is specially suited for table performance and is therefore included in this section.

THE EFFECT

The magician lays some objects on a table. He asks a person to select one mentally and remember it by name. Let us suppose that a pencil is chosen. The magician tells the person to turn his back and wait until the magician says: "Go."

With that word, the magician touches an object. The person mentally spells the first letter in the name of the selected object. In this case, he would repeat the letter "P" to himself.

The magician touches another object and says: "Go," for the second time. The person mentally declares the second letter, in this case "E." This is repeated, with the understanding that after the person has spelled the last letter in his word, he must call "Stop" and turn around.

Reaching "L" in pencil, the person says: "Stop." He looks around; to his surprise, the magician is touching the pencil, and all the witnesses testify to the fact that he had his hand on that object when the chooser called: "Stop."

THE METHOD

The trick works automatically, provided you choose the proper objects. These must be items that are each spelled with a different number of letters. For instance:

PIN	Three letters
DIME (or COIN)	Four letters
WATCH	Five letters
PENCIL	Six letters
PICTURE	Seven letters
ENVELOPE	Eight letters
CIGARETTE	Nine letters
FLASHLIGHT	Ten letters
HANDKERCHIEF	Twelve letters

When you first say: "Go," place your finger on any object. Do the same on the second count. On the third, however, touch the pin. If the person has chosen the pin, his mental spelling ends there, for "pin" has three letters.

Touch the coin for four; the watch for five and so on. Whatever object has been chosen, the spelling must end with it. Notice that the list contains no word with eleven letters. If the count goes that high, simply touch any object for eleven; but touch the handkerchief for twelve.

PRESENTATION

In presenting this trick, you may not always have the exact objects named in the list. Here are some alternates: KEY, 3. BOOK, PIPE, 4. CIGAR, PAPER, CLOCK, 5. BOTTLE, WALLET, 6. BLOTTER, ASH TRAY, 7. MAGAZINE, 8. TELEPHONE, 9. DICTIONARY, 10.

If you are forced to leave out any number it does not matter. Merely touch any object on that count, as with number eleven. But be sure never to have two objects that both spell with the same number of letters. You can reject any of these "duplicates" by saying that you have too many objects.

For the dinner table, you can use the following: CUP, 3. FORK, DISH, 4. KNIFE, GLASS, or SPOON, 5. SAUCER, NAPKIN, 6. These can be amplified with certain of the objects named in preceding lists. The trick, of course, is more natural if you begin by picking a few chance objects.

Give a brief demonstration of what you intend to do, by pointing out objects and explaining how the person is to spell mentally. In this preliminary, touch various objects in haphazard fashion, and end your spell at the wrong object.

Thus, while you explain what is to be done, so far as the words "Go" and "Stop" are concerned, you *do not* indicate what the result will be. That leaves the big surprise until the conclusion of the trick itself.

This trick may be repeated, but only once. It is not wise to repeat it at all if the spectators have watched you too closely when you touch the objects. You can throw them off by touching new objects on the first two counts; you may also introduce a few new items if you have the chance. These subterfuges will make a repetition possible with the average group of spectators. With too keen a group, however, avoid repetition.

The Magic Bank Roll

Another trick with a story. While the trick is good even when baldly presented, the tale that goes with it adds materially to its effectiveness.

THE EFFECT

The magician places a five dollar bill upon the table, pointing it away from him at an angle to the left. He lays a one dollar bill upon the five, but points the one dollar bill at right angles to the five, so that only the inner end of the five is covered by the inner end of the one.

The bills thus form a V, with the point toward the magician. Thereupon, the magician starts rolling the bills together, starting at the point and rolling them tightly *away* from him. He unrolls the bills, to show the one on top. He rolls them again and lets a person place a finger upon the one.

The magician places his left forefinger upon the projecting corner of the five and unrolls the bills with his right hand. To the utter amazement of all viewers, the five dollar bill is ABOVE the one dollar bill.

THE METHOD

The shift comes when the bills are almost completely rolled. Have your hands on the rolled centers. Point to the corner of the one dollar bill with your right hand and ask a spectator to place his finger upon it.

Your left hand is almost covering the last corner of the five dollar bill. Simply slide your left hand a few inches forward, pressing as you do so. With this movement, you slide the rolled up portion of the five so that its projecting corner comes underneath and flips over the top. This shift does the trick.

The movement is covered by the left hand, and the left forefinger must immediately press the corner of the five dollar bill against the table, while the right hand returns to the rolled up center. When the right hand unrolls the held bills, the five spot will be on top.

PRESENTATION

After noting the simple moves in this trick, practice it with patter. You need good reasons for the demonstration; and the following story supplies them.

"Here is a new game worked by gamblers. They lay two

bills of different denomination on the table and place one above the other. In this case, we shall use a one dollar bill over a five.

"The gamblers then roll the bills together. They ask people to bet which bill is on top. The man who calls the right bill wins." *Roll the bills as you explain this. Then start to unroll them, in ordinary fashion.*

"In this case, the one dollar bill wins, being on top. But the gamblers have a way to trap their victims. They start to roll the bills while a man is looking on; but they pretend not to see him.

"Here go the bills again; the one on top." *Roll the bills.* "Some one calls the victim. They ask him to bet on the top bill. Of course he chooses the one. Place your finger on it."

Address the last sentence to a spectator. As he puts his finger on the corner of the one dollar bill, make the shift. Nod toward your left finger as you place it on the corner of the five dollar bill.

"You are the victim; I am the gambler. Of course you have picked the one and are holding it; while I have the five, which I hold. That brings us to the surprise which the gamblers have prepared. When the bills are unrolled, the one spot is no longer on top. There is the five dollar bill, a winner!"

Diagrams, giving the positions of the bills for the "Magic Bank Roll," will be found with the illustration on page 49.

The Tricky Drinking Straws

Magicians will recognize this trick as an adaptation of one that has appeared in many forms; with paddles, matches, knives as objects used. In this version, drinking straws are the required items and they add a new touch to an old mystery; so different a touch that the trick will perplex the wisest observers.

THE EFFECT

The magician shows two drinking straws, encased in a paper wrapper. He tears a few inches from the end of the wrapper and presses the ends of the straws flat. He marks them with a blue pencil; then turns them over and marks the other sides with a red pencil.

Attention is then called to the wrapper which contains the drinking straws. A word is printed on the upper side; the magician points to it, calls attention to the red tips of the straws. He turns the straws over; the same word is printed on the other side. The magician points to the blue tips of the straws.

The magician passes his hand over the wrapper; gives it a turn. The word disappears leaving the wrapper blank. The spectators see the red tips of the straws. The magician turns the straws over to show the blue tips. The lower side of the wrapper is *also* blank. The words have completely gone.

The magician brings back the printed words. He shows them on both sides; they disappear again, both sides shown. They appear with the red tips of the drinking straws but not with the blue. After that, they arrive with the blue tips; but there is no longer any printing along with the red tips.

At this point, the magician decides to leave the wrapper as it is. He takes it from the straws, giving it for examination, showing its printing on one side only. As for the straws, they are also inspected and found to be quite ordinary.

THE METHOD

Let us consider this trick in simple form. Take a wrapper with two drinking straws. Hold it at one end between the thumb and forefinger of your right hand; the thumb on top. Turn your hand over, with a long, easy sweep, so that the fingers are uppermost.

At the same time slide your thumb to the right. The wrapper will make a half turn, so the same side remains upward. The revolution of the wrapper is not noticeable because of the longer sweep of the hand.

Reverse the manoeuver, turning the wrapper away from you as you tilt your right hand thumb uppermost. This time, slide the thumb to the left. The result will be another concealed half turn. The same side of the wrapper will be up.

It follows that you can show printing on *both* sides of the wrapper through this movement; or you can show both sides *blank*. You can show one side printed and the other side blank, by merely omitting the little movement of the thumb.

That is the old trick. The straws that are within the wrapper supply the new touch. When you begin the trick, tear away the far end of the wrapper. Press the straws flat; mark them with blue pencil. Turn the wrapper over; mark the other side of the straws red.

Proceed with the trick in the usual fashion. You will find that the straws behave in a helpful manner of their own. The straws have only *half* the diameter of the wrapper. Hence when it performs a *half* revolution under the pressure of your thumb, they do a *full* revolution.

Thus, when you are showing the wrapper to have printing on top and printing beneath, the straws are showing red on one side and blue on the other. An ordinary turn makes the wrapper blank instead of printed. It also shows the other side of the straws. But when you show the wrapper blank above, blank below, the straws alternate by revealing red and blue just as they did previously.

By varying your twists, you can show printing with the blue tips; blank wrapper with the red. Then printing with the blues, with the reds; after that, blank wrapper with the blues and printing with the reds only.

By taking the wrapper from the straws at the finish, you can let the items be examined, but they will no longer be in shape for any one else to try the trick. The spectators will be utterly baffled.

The actions of the straws *look* normal; for they *always* change from red and blue just as they should do. This offsets the mysterious behavior of the wrapper which changes at will. Spectators can not explain one because of the other. That is why you will find this trick far superior to the old "turn over" stunts, which—despite their attempts at novelty—were always the same old trick.

PRESENTATION

Suit the patter to your own way of performing the trick, as you will find that your routine will vary according to your audience. The following remarks can be utilized as an outline.

"Here are some drinking straws; to identify them, I shall mark their tips with a blue pencil. Wait! I almost forgot; the straws have another side, so I shall mark them red underneath.

"Notice this wrapper with its printed words. You see it is printed on the top and on the bottom also. Since we can't tell the bottom from the top, we can say that it is printed on the side that has the red-tipped straws. And also, you see, on the side that has the blue-tipped straws.

"Watch that printing vanish. A sweep of the straws; it is gone from the red side. There was printing on the blue side, wasn't there? To make the job complete, we find it gone from that side too. Gone from the red; gone from the blue. Back with the red; and back with the blue.

"Let's try it half and half. There is printing with the blues but not with the reds. Still with the blues. What's this? It's back with the reds. That means it must be gone from the blues. There you are. Blank with the blues. The printing must have jumped right through the straws.

"Yet when you take a look at the wrapper, you find that it is ordinary printing. Here, look at the wrapper, just as it is. One side printed, one side blank. As for the straws, they are the same as ever. Here is one; it has a red tip and a blue. So has the other. Unfortunately, they are no longer first class drinking straws."

COMMENT

A double pencil, red at one end, blue at the other, is useful to have on hand when you show this trick. If colored pencils are not available, use a black one; mark the straws on one side and leave them blank on the other. Change the patter accordingly.

Use of red and blue is advised because the colors are effective and leave no doubt regarding the fact that you turn the straws over every time. The only practice needed is a brief experiment to learn the proper amount of the turn.

Proper pressure will make the straws do their turn inside the wrapper which is loose. In a sense, you keep the wrapper in a stationary position, but revolve the straws inside it. A test with straws and wrapper shows how naturally it works.

If the only available wrapper is a blank one, mark it with letters in red and blue, on one side. If a wrapper has different printing on each side, change the printing instead of making one side blank.

With wrappers printed the same on both sides, make colored pencil marks on one side before you show the trick.

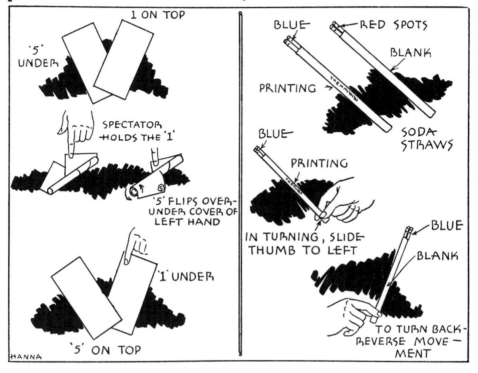

| How the bills are placed for the "Magic Bank Roll" | Illustrating the correct moves with the "Tricky Drinking Straws" |

CARD MAGIC

Card tricks are always popular, particularly when they present points of novelty. The tricks in this section are all unusual and there are enough of them to make a complete program of this type of magic.

Certain of these tricks are specially suited for the card table. You can show them while persons are all about you, watching at the closest possible range. Others are meant for regular performance, where you have the table set up away from the audience, in preparation for your program.

Both types of tricks are effective; and you can use certain card tricks in other programs as well. You will find, when you try them, that good card tricks are welcome items in any routine of magic.

TRICKS IN THIS SECTION

King, Queen and Jack
The Poker Deal
The Turn-Over Card
The Tricky Joker
The Night Club Mystery
The Penetrated Card
Cards and Glasses
The Fifth Card

King, Queen, Jack

This is a novelty in card dealing tricks, as it requires the assistance of three spectators and taxes the magician with a seemingly difficult problem.

THE EFFECT

The magician takes a king, a queen and a jack from a pack of cards. He lays these on the table and invites three persons to each take one of the cards. They are to choose among themselves which card each will take, and no one is to inform the magician which person has the king, queen or jack.

The persons pocket their cards, or place them out of sight. The magician returns and picks up the rest of the pack. To the first person, he gives one card; to the second, three cards; to the third, five cards.

The magician states that the person who holds the king is to take the pack and remove the same number of cards that he was just given. The person who holds the queen is to take *twice* the number that the performer just gave him. The person with the jack is to take *five times* as many cards as he just received.

The magician departs so that the cards may be taken in his absence. He returns and picks up what remains of the pack. He deals these left-over cards in three heaps. Pointing to the spectators one by one, the magician names the person who holds the king; also the one who has the queen; and finally, the person who took the jack.

In each case, the magician is correct.

THE METHOD

This trick depends upon a simple system; by merely dealing the left over cards, you can tell where the king, queen and jack are located.

Deal the cards in three heaps; one card at a time. Count them as you do so. When you come to number 11, skip a heap (placing it on the right instead of the center, as you deal from left to right). Count that card as number 11, however.

When you come to number 22, again skip a heap (placing the card on the right instead of the center). Count that card as number 22 and continue right along with the deal. Numbers 11 and 22 are your key numbers.

The heaps represent the three persons. Where the deal ends, is your clue to the person who holds the queen. If you finish on the first heap, the first person has the queen; the second heap, second person; third heap, third person.

The number of remaining cards gives you the clue to the jack. If the total of cards dealt is less than eleven (your first key number), the third person holds the jack. If it is more than eleven but LESS than twenty-two, the second person has the jack. If it is twenty-two or over, the first person is the one with the jack.

The king, of course, must be with the person who holds neither the queen nor the jack. You need no further clue to the king.

PRESENTATION

Present this trick as a problem in divination. Be sure to specify the important facts. Spectators are to take the king, queen and jack as they agree; and to put those cards away. When you give them one, three and five cards respectively, they are to consider those numbers alone, not counting king, queen or jack with them.

Regard the person to your left as the first person and give him ONE card. The person in front of you is the second. Give him THREE cards. The person to your right is the third person. Give him FIVE cards.

Make it clear that whoever has the king is to take the same amount of cards that YOU gave him. The person with the queen is to take TWICE as many; the person with the jack FIVE times as many. Do not refer to the numbers one, three and five, as amounts that you passed to the three people.

In making the deal with the left-over cards, keep counting carefully and deal slowly. Hold the numbers 11 and 22 in mind, so that you will remember to pass over a heap when you come to either of those key numbers. After the deal, study the heaps carefully.

You mentally figure the queen's position first; the jack's next; and the king's last. But in pointing out the spectators, first name the one who holds the king; then the holder of the queen; finally the person who has the jack.

COMMENT

This trick MUST be performed with a full pack of EXACTLY fifty-two cards. Since you give the spectators three to begin with (king, queen and jack); then nine (one, three and five cards), you have just forty cards for the actual trick.

For purposes of reference, the possible results are given herewith in table form. A, B and C represent the holders of the three cards: first, second and third person.

Table of Combinations.

First:

> A—King. B—Queen. C—Jack.
> A takes 1; B takes 6; C takes 25. Total 32.
> Cards left for magician's deal: 8.

Second:

> A—Queen. B—King. C—Jack.
> A takes 2; B takes 3; C takes 25. Total 30.
> Cards left for magician's deal: 10.

Third:

> A—King. B—Jack. C—Queen.
> A takes 1; B takes 15; C takes 10. Total 26.
> Cards left for magician's deal: 14.

Fourth:

> A—Queen. B—Jack. C—King.
> A takes 2; B takes 15; C takes 5. Total 22.
> Cards left for magician's deal: 18.

Fifth:

> A—Jack. B—King. C—Queen.
> A takes 5; B takes 3; C takes 10. Total 18.
> Cards left for magician's deal: 22.

Sixth:

> A—Jack. B—Queen. C—King.
> A takes 5; B takes 6; C takes 5. Total 16.
> Cards left for magician's deal: 24.

NOTE: No skip deal in first and second combinations.
   Skip a heap with number 11 in third and fourth.
   Skip heaps with 11 and 22 in fifth and sixth.
   First and second combinations: Less than 11, signifying Jack with C.
   Third and fourth combinations: Less than 22, signifying Jack with B.
   Fifth and sixth combinations: 22 or over, signifying Jack with A.

The Poker Deal

All performers of card tricks are asked if they know how big hands can be dealt in a card game. This trick is the best answer to that question. Through this method, any one can deal remarkable hands over and over, with a show of seemingly great skill. Yet the trick requires no skill whatever.

THE EFFECT

Taking a pack of cards, the magician deals two hands; one card at a time, three cards in each group. He always gets three jacks in the heap on the left. After a few repetitions, he deals hands of *five* cards each. The first hand dealt shows bigger combinations; full hands of three jacks and two aces, or three aces and two jacks.

After demonstrating that such hands can be dealt whenever chosen, the magician supplies a climax by dealing two hands and turning them up. The first hand, the opponent's, holds four jacks. The second hand, the magician's, tops it with FOUR ACES.

THE METHOD

Arrange the top nine cards of the pack in the following order, counting from top down:

Jack, Jack, Jack, Odd Card, Jack, Red Ace, Red Ace, Ace of Clubs, Ace of Spades.

Start by dealing left, right, card by card, until you have dealt two heaps of three cards each. As you deal the third card to the heap on the right, do not drop it; instead, slide it *beneath* the two cards on the table. Lift all three together and replace them on top of the pack.

All the cards have naturally been dealt faces down. Since you do not intend to show the hand on the right, this slide under system is the easiest way to pick it up and replace it on the pack, keeping the faces down. You follow this same system all through the trick.

Turn up the heap on the table. Show that it contains three jacks. Place the three jacks faces downward on the pack. Repeat the deal just as you did before, scooping the second hand and putting it back on the pack. Again, you will have three jacks in the first heap.

This will repeat indefinitely, for the FOURTH jack is alternating in with the others. This is an old trick and a good one; but it has no climax. Hence, you merely repeat it three or four times as a preliminary to the bigger trick that is to come.

Deal FIVE cards in each heap. The fifth card of the second heap goes beneath it as usual and serves to pick up that hand

and put it face downward on the pack. Turn up the first hand and show it. Repeat the trick; but from now on, ALWAYS with five cards for each hand.

The hands on the left will vary with different deals; but most of them will be large ones. They must be displayed faces up; replaced faces down on the pack without disturbing their order. Then comes the next deal. There will be nine of these hands altogether and their order and appearance will be as follows:

(1)   Full House (Three Jacks, Two Aces).
(2)   Full House (Three Jacks, Two Aces).
(3)   Full House (Three Aces, Two Jacks).
(4)   Incomplete Hand (Three Aces, One Jack).
(5)   Full House (Three Aces, Two Jacks).
(6)   Incomplete Hand (Three Aces, One Jack).
(7)   Incomplete Hand (Two Aces, Two Jacks).
(8)   Incomplete Hand (Two Aces, Two Jacks).
(9)   Four Jacks in   First Hand.
       Four Aces in YOUR Hand.

NOTE: The hands termed "incomplete" have five cards like the others, but one card is the odd one—neither an ace nor a jack.

On the ninth deal, which finishes the trick, the second hand dealt is NOT replaced upon the pack. Simply slide the fifth card under it and leave it there to be levered up for the climax, when your hand as well as the first one, is shown.

It will be noted that four of the nine big hands are incomplete. They must necessarily be so to keep the deal automatic. The occurrence of those hands must be explained, and that is taken care of by means of proper patter. The whole routine is presented as a story, which explains all the hands.

PRESENTATION

Hold the pack as though about to deal. Begin a brief preliminary story and proceed with the following talk.

"There was once a wise old gambler who had a method of dealing that was all his own. He used to practice it by dealing two hands of three cards each, like this."

Deal two hands. Replace the right on the pack. Show the left heap; replace it.

"The wise old gambler always turned up three jacks. He put them on top of the pack again and dealt them over." *Deal again.* "There they were. The three jacks, back again." *Replace.*

"The mystery was how the old gambler could always bring that third jack." *Continue three card deal.* "Other gamblers watched him; kept looking for him to slip. But the three jacks always arrived. The system never failed."

THREE CARD DEAL

FIVE CARD DEAL

THE LIFT

TOP CARDS OF PACK

Continue with the three card deal while you go on with the story.

"One day a young gambler spent hours watching the wise old bloke. Every time the three jacks turned up, the young fellow was goggle-eyed. At last he thought he would make some criticism. He waited until the old gambler had finished a deal."

Here, you complete the LAST of your three jack deals. Replace the three jacks on the pack and pause in dealing while you add:

"The young gambler said that three cards were not enough for a hand. He asked the old gambler what he would do if he dealt a full poker hand of five cards. The old gambler said: 'I'll show you. This is what I would give the other player along with the three jacks'."

Deal the first five card hand. Show the full house; Jacks over Aces.

"Up turned a full house. The young gambler was amazed. He asked the old gambler if he could deal *that* hand again. The old chap said: 'Certainly'."

Deal the second five card hand.

"'There you are', said the old gambler, 'another full house. But when I deal full houses, I like to give good measure'. So the old gambler dealt the cards again."

Deal the third five card hand.

"This time he showed a full house with aces over jacks. He handed the pack to the young gambler and asked him to try it. The young fellow did; but he missed on one card."

Deal the fourth five card hand.

"The old gambler shook his head. He said: 'You need another jack, young fellow. Here's the way to get it.' So he dealt the cards again." *Deal the fifth five card hand.* "There was the full house back again, aces over jacks."

Pick up the cards; hold them as you continue:

"The young gambler thought he had the system, because he had only missed on one card. So he tried it again." *Deal the sixth five card hand.* "But he missed. There was the odd card instead of the jack. He went after them again." *Deal the seventh five card hand.* "This time he managed to get two pair; but there was the same odd card to spoil the full house. He gave it one last try." *Deal the eighth five card hand.* "Once again, two pair, with the odd card right in the middle."

Pick up the hand, prepare for the ninth and last deal. Your cue to this is the ODD card in the middle of the hand. Continue with the story.

"The young gambler admitted he was licked. But he wanted to know how he could get rid of the one card he didn't want. The old gambler said: 'Why get rid of it? Watch'."

Deal the NINTH five card hand. This time, as you start to lever up the heap on the right, leave it on the table. Pick up the first hand dealt; spread it face up and say:

"With that, the old gambler turned up FOUR JACKS. He said that the hand was better than a full house; that there was no need to eliminate the odd card. The young gambler came through with one objection. He asked: 'But isn't that hand too good for the other player? How are you going to beat him when he holds four jacks'?"

" 'Easily enough', replied the wise old gambler. 'Take a look at my hand and see what I dealt for myself.' "

Turn up the hand on the right; spread the cards and show that your own hand contains the FOUR ACES.

COMMENT

Properly presented, this trick is highly effective, and the correct presentation naturally depends upon the story. Do not, however, attempt to learn the patter word for word. You can pause at intervals; change your speed of deal as you require. Simply insert the important remarks where they belong.

The use of the story makes the spectators think that you *purposely* dealt the incomplete hands. Therefore, you should give the patter in your own individual manner; but with emphasis on the important points as outlined.

The Turn-Over Card

The discovery of a chosen card is a basic type of card trick. To be effective, such a trick should have a surprising climax and should seem to offset any manipulative efforts on the part of the magician. The following trick fulfills those qualifications, particularly since a large portion of the action is performed by a spectator instead of the magician.

THE EFFECT

The magician takes any pack of cards; gives it to a spectator and asks for a thorough shuffle. After the shuffle, the person is told to cut the pack in two heaps; to keep one for himself and give the other to the magician.

The magician turns his back. He asks the spectator to look at the top card of his—the spectator's—heap; to remember the card and leave it face down on the heap. That done, the magician turns about and drops his half of the pack upon the spectator's cards. He lets the spectator hold the entire pack.

Next, the magician instructs the spectator to put the pack behind his back; to remove the top card and insert it somewhere in the center. He tells him to take the next card from the top of the pack; to turn it *face upward* behind his back and thrust it somewhere in the pack.

That done, the cards are given to the magician. He remarks that two cards are important and can be easily found. One is the card noted by the spectator; the other, the card that the spectator placed face upward in the pack. The magician announces that these cards will be found together.

The pack is spread on the table. The magician arrives at a face up card. He pulls out the card just below it. He asks the name of the card noted by the spectator. The magician turns the card face up; it is the right one.

THE METHOD

When you turn your back, you must perform an action with the half of the pack that you hold. Turn the bottom card of that packet face upward. Do the same with the card that is *second* from the top.

The packet appears ordinary when you drop it on the spectator's half; but actually, you have a card face up, just above the one he noted; for his card is the top one of his heap; and the bottom card of your packet is face upward.

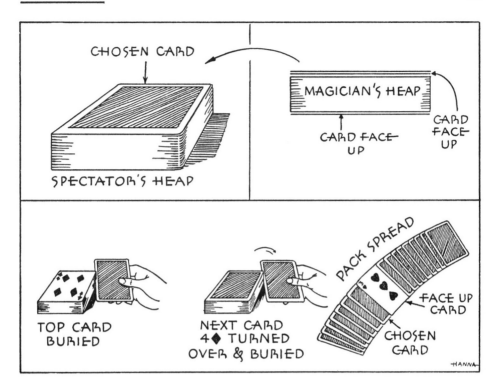

CHOSEN CARD

MAGICIAN'S HEAP

CARD FACE UP

CARD FACE UP

SPECTATOR'S HEAP

TOP CARD BURIED

NEXT CARD 4♦ TURNED OVER & BURIED

PACK SPREAD

FACE UP CARD

CHOSEN CARD

HANNA

You also have another card face up; the one that lies second from the top. Since the pack is squared, it will not be noticed.

Give the spectator the whole pack. Have him put it behind his back and insert the top card anywhere. Then tell him to turn the second card *face up* and insert it in the pack. He reverses the card; but does not see it, since the pack is behind his back.

The spectator *thinks* that he is turning a card *face up;* actually, he is turning it *face down,* for you saw to it that the card was face up. Thus, when the pack is spread, the spectator looks for a face up card, believing that it must be the one he inserted somewhere.

He sees one face up card. It locates the one that he previously noted. Since it is the only face up card in the entire pack, the spectator never suspects that it was set face up beforehand. He—and all the others present—are amazed by the startling coincidence.

PRESENTATION

The trick should be presented in a casual manner. After the spectator takes a heap, you can tell him to shuffle it; then look at the top card. Step well away; no one will think of the half of the pack that you have retained. You will find no difficulty in reversing the cards.

When you return, place your half of the pack on the spectator's and leave the cards in his hands. Move him to a corner; tell him to put his hands behind his back, with the pack. Tell him to bury one card; stress that the next must be turned face upward, then inserted.

As soon as these actions are done, you are safe. Become more deliberate. Tell the spectator to place the pack on the table. Remind him that he has done everything; that he noted a card and buried another face up in the pack.

State confidently that you will produce a startling coincidence by bringing the two cards together. Spread the pack slowly; find the face up card. Deliberately draw out the one below it; ask the name of the noted card.

Pause long enough to impress the spectators; then repeat the name of the card and turn it face up.

The Tricky Joker

This is a 'spelling trick' with cards, that provides a mysterious finale. It was originated by Frank L. Thomas, who gave the author the explanation, for publication in a book on magic.

THE EFFECT

The magician holds a small stack of cards, face down. He takes the top card and transfers it to the bottom, spelling the letter "A," aloud. The next card is transferred, with the letter "C;" a third card is transferred, with the letter "E." Having spelled "Ace," the magician turns up the next card on top of the stack. The card is an Ace.

Placing the ace face up on the table, the magician spells "T-W-O," moving a card from top to bottom with each letter. He then says "Two;" and turns up a two-spot. Laying the deuce face up on the table, he spells "T-H-R-E-E," a card for each letter; and turns up a three on the next card.

So far, the trick resembles the oldest of all spelling tricks, in which the cards are spelled out from Ace to King. But when the magician has spelled "F-O-U-R," a surprise is forthcoming. On the next card, he turns up a joker instead of a four.

Somewhat surprised, the magician turns the joker face down on the stack. He resumes his spelling by again announcing "F-O-U-R." With the word "Four," he turns up the required four spot. From then on, cards are spelled in regular rotation, until the magician arrives at "Nine." Thereupon, the joker appears again.

Turning the joker face down on the stack, the magician patiently respells "N-I-N-E" and announces "Nine." This time the nine arrives. The magician spells the ten spot with no interference from the joker; but he strikes a real problem with the Jack. The Joker comes up instead; the magician turns it down and spells "J-A-C-K;" but when the next card is turned up, it is again the Joker.

To offset this situation, the magician decides to fool the Joker. Instead of spelling "Jack," he spells "Joker." The magician turns up the next card; it proves to be the Jack. Laying the Jack face up on the table, he states that he still has the Queen and King to spell, so it would be best to eliminate the Joker. So the magician spells "J-O-K-E-R" and turns up the Joker on the next card.

Having thus made the Joker behave, the magician puts the troublesome card in his pocket. He then spells the word "Queen" and turns up the Queen. This leaves him with only one card.

The magician states that the card is the King; but of course it is impossible to spell it, with only a single card. Instead, he will simply turn it face up and let every one see it.

The magician turns the card face up; but instead of being the King, it is the Joker! Reaching in his pocket, the magician finds that the card he put there was the King. The tricky Joker somehow managed to get back in the game.

THE METHOD

This trick depends, of course, upon a special arrangement, or "set-up"; but it also requires an extra joker, taken from a duplicate pack. The magician uses fourteen cards in the stack; and the two jokers are among them. The King is never in the stack. It is placed in the coat pocket, beforehand.

Here is your arrangement, running from the top card to the bottom: 8, 10, 5, Ace, 7, Joker, 9, 2, 6, Jack, 4, Joker, Queen, 3. This order is fixed with the cards face down, the eight on the top; the three, lowermost.

Simply move the cards from top to bottom as you spell; each time you name a card and turn it face up, toss it on the table. The Joker will arrive instead of the Four. Do not remove it: place it face down on top of the packet and repeat the spell of Four, to obtain the actual Four.

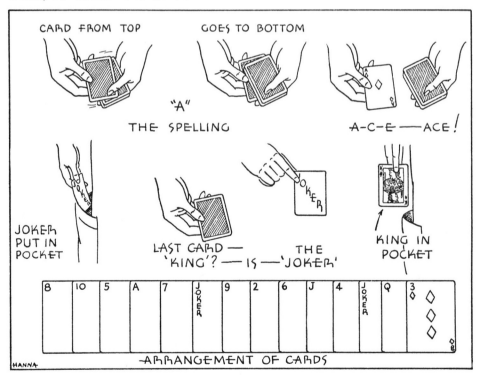

The same procedure governs the Nine, when the Joker arrives instead of it. When you come to the Jack, however, the situation is different. The Joker turns up; when you turn it down on top of the packet, you have four cards. Since "Jack" is spelled with four letters, the fifth card (turned up) will always be the Joker, however often you repeat.

That is why you spell "Joker" instead of Jack, pretending that your purpose is to outwit the Joker. When the Jack comes up, toss it on the table. Then spell "Joker" over again. You place this Joker in your pocket. When you do so, feel for the King, and place the Joker on the *inner* side of the pocket.

Spell "Queen" and turn up the Queen, which will arrive automatically. Then announce that you hold the King; that you will turn it face up. Do so and show the second Joker. The King should be held in the left hand, so that the right can go at once to the pocket and bring out the King as promptly as if it were the only card there.

PRESENTATION

Since the bulk of the presentation is the actual spelling of the cards, there is no need for much additional patter. Simply insert the remarks that concern the Joker, as described in the preceding paragraphs.

By the time you have neared the finish of the trick, the spectators will be so used to the spelling that they will take it for granted that you have the King in the stack; in fact, they will almost believe that they have seen it there.

That is why the finish produces such a surprise. Pretend to be as baffled as the spectators. Reach into your pocket and seize the King in a hurry, as though it were the card that you put away only a few moments previously. No one will begin to guess that a second Joker was used.

Remember that a card must be shifted from top to bottom on each letter that you spell; that you must call each card by its value at the end of each spell and turn it up as you call it. Deal off all such cards; but always turn the Joker face down on top of the pack, when it arrives by mistake.

When you spell the Joker by its right name and obtain it, then you remove it like the other cards; but it goes into your pocket; not on the table.

COMMENT

Other spelling tricks have been designed that resemble this one; but in every case, they require sleight-of-hand. This method eliminates all "changes" or "switches" that require skill, as the substitution of King for Joker takes place in the pocket.

The Night Club Mystery

This is a story with a pack of cards. It has appeared with many variations, each dependent on its own particular patter. It is always effective, as it carries a puzzling feature that gives it the appearance of a trick. Since the story is essential, it will be described in patter form.

THE EFFECT

The magician holds a batch of cards, faces down, in his left hand. He holds the Jack of Hearts in his right hand, face up. Calling attention to the Jack of Hearts, the magician states:

"This young chap worked at a night club. He felt that his services were worth thirty-five dollars a week and he told that to his boss. The boss said that business was bad; so the smart young lad decided that he would improve it. He went out to dig up some customers."

The magician places the jack on top of the pack. He cuts the cards, begins to deal them face up, one at a time, stating:

"He was gone one minute, two minutes, three minutes"— *counting a card for each minute*—"four minutes, five minutes"—

The magician stops the deal; states:

"Then he came back."

The magician turns up the jack and deals it by itself. He picks up the other cards, turns them faces down and places them BENEATH the pack.

"With him, he brought three big business men."

The magician deals three kings beside the jack.

"They liked the night club; but they felt lonely. One of them called the young chap over and said: 'Here's ten dollars'," *The magician deals a ten spot with the kings.* "Call up some of your girl friends and invite them over."

The magician replaces the jack on top of the pack, leaving the kings and the ten spot on the table. He cuts the pack, saying:

"The young fellow went out and made a phone call. He was gone one minute, two minutes, three minutes, four minutes"— *dealing a card for each minute*—"then he came back."

The magician deals the jack face up. He picks up the batch he just dealt; places them beneath the pack.

"Right after that, the girls arrived. Three of them." *The magician deals three queens.* "Right after that, a waiter entered carrying a tray." *The magician turns up a three spot (a trey) and deals it with the queens.* "On the tray was a telegram for one of the big business brains. It was two dollars, collect, so the business man paid it."

The magician deals a two spot.

"The telegram was from a salesman, saying he would arrive in town on the next train. So the big business man called our young friend over and said: 'Here's five dollars. Go down to the station and meet this fellow.'" *The magician deals a five spot.* "So the young chap started for the station."

The magician replaces the jack on top of the pack. He cuts the pack; deals cards faces up, counting:

"One minute, two minutes, three minutes, four minutes, five minutes"—*The magician pauses.* "The young chap came back." *The magician deals the jack; picks up the cards just dealt and puts them beneath.* "With him was the salesman." *The magician deals a king.* "As soon as he joined the party, the salesman observed that there were only three girls. He called the young chap over and said: 'Here's five dollars. Call up another girl'." *The magician deals a five spot.* "So the young chap went out again."

The jack is replaced on the pack. The cards are cut. The magician deals cards faces up, counting:

"One minute, two minutes, three minutes"—

The magician stops; and adds:

"The young chap came back." *He deals the jack. He picks up the three cards just dealt and places them beneath the pack.* "He brought along another girl." *The magician deals a queen.* "But she didn't like the party. She said to our young friend: 'Here's five dollars. Dig up some of your own friends.'"—*the magician deals a five spot*—"so the young chap made another trip."

The jack goes back on the pack. The cards are cut. The magician counts as he deals cards faces up:

"One minute, two minutes, three minutes—the young lad returned."

The magician deals the jack. He puts the cards just dealt back beneath the pack.

"With him, he had the boys from Brooklyn. Three of his old pals." *The magician deals three jacks.* "They proved to be the life of the party. The big business men went home; the salesman went to his hotel. But then came trouble. The boys from Brooklyn had to settle up the bill.

"It was eighteen dollars; all they had was a couple of two dollar bills." *The magician deals two deuces.* "But two of the boys had check books, so each wrote out a check for seven dollars." *The magician deals two sevens.* "That settled the matter. Everybody left happy.

"Then the young chap asked his boss: 'Do I get my thirty-five a week'? The boss said: 'Sure. Here's your first pay, in advance.' So he gave him ten, fifteen, twenty-five, thirty-five."

With these last numbers, the magician deals four cards: a ten, a five, a ten and a ten. He has no cards left.

The tale is finished.

THE METHOD

The cards are arranged beforehand. Knowing the order, you simply follow the story and remember the important details. The arrangement is as follows:

King, king, king, ten, queen, queen, queen, three, two, five, king, five, queen, five, jack, jack, jack, two, two, seven, seven, ten, five, ten, ten.

The jack of hearts is separate from the arrangement. Also you must remember the bottom card—the last ten—by its suit. It should preferably be the ten of diamonds and it serves you as a key card.

When you put the jack of hearts on top of the packet and cut the cards, you place the jack at some unknown position. When you deal the cards faces up, counting the minutes, you watch for your key card. When you see the ten of diamonds, you stop, making it the *last minute* counted.

The *next* card will be the jack of hearts. You deal it as you state that the young chap has returned. *Always* pick up the cards just dealt and put them beneath, so your key card, the ten of diamonds, will again be on the bottom.

You deal the three kings; then a ten spot. Put the jack of hearts on top of the pack; cut and start to count the minutes, watching for the key ten of diamonds. End the minute count as before. This time, the jack of hearts is followed by three queens, a trey, a two and a five.

Repeat the usual procedure, counting minutes to your key card. This time the jack is followed by a king and a five. Another replacement of the jack; the minute count; the jack arrives followed by a queen and a five.

The next replacement is the last. The minute count brings the jack of hearts. It is followed by the other three jacks, two deuces, two sevens; and finally a ten, a five and two tens. That exhausts the cards and the story is ended.

PRESENTATION

While this trick requires absolutely no skill, it must be practiced and rehearsed so that you can run through it smoothly. You have to remember the story; but you can vary the patter slightly, so there is no need to memorize it word for word.

The spectators are mystified because you *always* know when the jack of hearts is due back. The fact that the number of minutes differ does not injure this feature. Frequently, a certain number of minutes are repeated, which increases the effect.

It is always best to cut deep; particularly at the outset of the story, when you have a large number of cards. A deep cut places few cards on top of the jack and makes the minute count shorter.

You can ask some one else to cut the pack, after the first or second cut. If he only cuts a few cards, cut a few more yourself. *Single cuts* do not disturb the arrangement. The rotation of the cards will *always* be the same. The cut merely brings the key card above the jack of hearts.

For a neat beginning to the trick, you can practice a special cut. Hold the cards between the left thumb (at the left) and the last three fingers (at the right). Have your forefinger beneath, at the outer end of the pack.

Hold the right hand at the inner end. Press your left forefinger against the outer ends of the lowermost cards; catch the cards with the finger nail and snap the forefinger inward. This will shoot the bottom cards into the right hand, which immediately places them on top of the pack.

It looks as though the cards have cut themselves; and this adds to the effectiveness of the trick. If you find this automatic cut easy to do, use it. If not, simply cut the cards by drawing some from the bottom with your right hand and placing them on top.

The Penetrated Card

This is an excellent trick to use with any card routine as its effect is quite different from that of most card tricks. It forms a novelty in any program.

THE EFFECT

The magician shows a small folder made of cardboard, large enough to encase a playing card. The folder is double, folding upward at the bottom. The front half contains three openings like little windows. Between the two upper openings is a small hole.

Taking a six spot of diamonds, the magician places it behind the openings, so that each set of spots shows through. He folds up the rear portion of the folder; then places rubber bands around the folder, to keep the card inside.

The magician shows the back of the folder; there, the spectators see a tiny hole that corresponds to the one in front. Showing the front of the folder again, the magician calls attention to the spots on the card.

Taking a match, he pushes it through the folder from in back. Since the match goes through the small hole, it naturally penetrates the playing card. To make this a certainty, the magician can push a small string through the folder and draw it back and forth.

Once the string is clear, he shows the folder from both sides, then removes the rubber bands. The card slides out and is given to the spectators. To their surprise, they find it undamaged. The penetration has apparently been accomplished in magical fashion.

THE METHOD

This trick is simply and effectively accomplished thanks to a special preparation of the folder that receives the card. Printed on one side of the rear half are two spots that resemble those on a six of diamonds.

This is the side that should be kept *away from view* when the folder is first exhibited. Since the back section of the folder dangles, no one can see the printed spots. If placed upon a table, the opened folder should be laid with the spots *downward*.

Holding the opened folder toward the audience, with your left hand, pick up the six of diamonds with your right. Show the face of the card to the spectators; place it directly in back of the three windows. Fold up the bottom half of the folder, bringing it in back of the playing card.

The printed spots are hidden from view. You keep the card in its position by pressing the front and back of the folder. Put a rubber band around the folder; as you do so, turn the folder so that the spectators can see the back. Gird the folder with a second rubber band.

When you reach for a third rubber band, release pressure. The card will slide down to the folded edge of the folder. Should it stick, press the sides of the folder and the playing card will make its trip, for the folder is wider than the card.

Since the front of the folder is turned in your direction, you can see when the card is properly in place. To all appearances, it will seem to be at its original position, for the printed spots inside the folder back are now visible. They APPEAR to be the top two spots belonging to the six of diamonds.

Turn the front of the folder toward the spectators. Push the match through the double hole; a simple matter, for it goes ABOVE the top edge of the card. Repeat the manoeuver with a piece of string. After you have thus "penetrated" the card, you are ready for the finish.

Remove the rubber bands, turning the folder upside down as you do so. Keep the back of the folder toward the spectators. The card will slide to your hand; you can immediately give it for inspection. Then, still holding the folder back toward the audience, raise the front half.

As a final touch, you can place one hand over the printed spots and thus turn the folder so that the spectators see the interior. Two fingers will cover the spots; or if your thumb is a wide one, you may easily lay it across them.

Since you merely wish to prove that there is nothing inside the folder, only a brief display is necessary. Persons will not suspect another card inside the folder, for its presence would not account for the penetration. You can close the folder at the finish and lay it with the windows down; and the creased edge toward the audience.

Or, if persons are close enough to pick up the folder, simply pocket it after the trick is finished.

PRESENTATION

This trick should be presented as directly as possible; but in a deliberate fashion. Take your time, to show that all is fair. The following patter will serve as an outline.

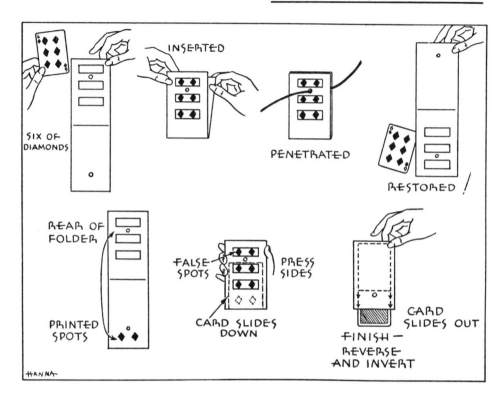

"I shall use a playing card to demonstrate a scientific experiment that has been classed as remarkable. Any card will do; suppose I use this six spot of diamonds. I want you to examine it beforehand and afterward.

"Here is a little cardboard folder, just about large enough to hold the playing card. I place the card behind these openings. Notice that the spots show through. All that we need now are some rubber bands to keep the card from becoming excited and jumping out of its temporary prison.

"Notice the small hole in the front of the folder. There is one just like it, here at the back, so the two form a straight route through. That will prove important before we have finished.

"Here is the card facing you again. The next object that we require is a wooden match; a solid stick, despite its small size. I place the match through the double hole. There it comes, puncturing the card.

"Since the hole is now a perfect tunnel, we can use it for transportation purposes. This string will represent a streamliner coming through the tunnel. Back and forth; then out again.

"So far, we have forgotten the scientific purpose of this experiment. That is, you have forgotten it; not I. You have seen objects pass through the playing card. Therefore, the card itself should show evidence of their passage in the form of a small hole. The scientific part of the experiment is the suppression of the evidence.

"Let us remove the card. Here. Look at it. Where is the hole? It isn't. Just another one of Einstein's fourth dimension theories, put into actual practice. There are the holes in the folder, where the match and the string went through. They went through the card, too, but it is still intact; and that's the magic of it."

> The folder necessary for this trick is printed, ready to be cut out, upon one of the cardboard inserts in this volume. The printed spots are identical with those on most makes of playing cards. Should you prefer another style of card, cut a strip from a seven spot of diamonds and gum it over the printed spots that appear on the folder. The spots will then match those of your own six of diamonds.

Cards and Glasses

Used in a program of miscellaneous magic, this trick is a distinct novelty. It is also an excellent climax to a regular card routine; but it must be presented as part of an act, not simply as a trick at the card table.

THE EFFECT

The magician removes two cards from a pack and places each in a separate drinking glass. He turns the tumblers so that the cards face the audience. One card is the four of hearts; the other, the ten of diamonds.

Showing two pieces of newspaper, the magician places one around the glass that contains the ten of diamonds; he fastens the paper with pins or paper clips, so that it forms a cylinder. He starts to do the same with the glass that contains the four of hearts; but the piece of paper is too small; so he simply reverses the glass, turning the back of the card toward the spectators.

The magician commands the cards to change places. He uncovers the first glass; reveals the four of hearts instead of the ten of diamonds. He removes this card; turns around the glass that has a card back to the audience. The card in the second glass is no longer the four of hearts; it has become the ten of diamonds.

The cards and the glasses are given for examination, to prove that they are quite ordinary. In fact, the trick may be worked with a borrowed pack.

THE METHOD

Although the pack is an ordinary one, you must have a special card of your own. This is double-faced, showing the ten of diamonds on one side; the four of hearts on the other.

Take any pack; place this card on the bottom, so that the ten of diamonds shows. On top of the pack put the real ten of diamonds, with the four of hearts just beneath it.

To begin the trick, pick up the pack and lift off both top cards. Press the sides between thumb and forefinger, so that the cards bend. This makes them appear as one card; when you place them in the glass, the curved wall of the tumbler takes care of the needed pressure.

The bend should be made so that the faces of the cards are concave. To all appearances, you have placed just one card—the four of hearts—in the glass.

TWO AS ONE

DOUBLE FACE CARD

GLASS REVERSED

TAKING FRONT CARD

FAKE CARD

REAL CARD

TURN PAPER AROUND

—HANNA—

From the bottom of the pack, remove the fake ten of diamonds, keeping its diamond face toward the audience. Place it in the other glass and circle the glass with a sheet of paper. As you adjust the paper into a cylinder and fix it in place, turn the glass half around, so that the other side of the double-faced card will be toward the spectators when the tumbler is uncovered.

You start to cover the glass that holds the two cards; but find the paper cylinder too small. That is something which you saw to, beforehand, as you need an excuse to turn the glass around. Pick up the glass with the right hand, then turn it so the back of the card is to the audience. As you do so, hold the discarded paper in your left hand and bring the glass in back of it.

The position of the left hand is important. It should hold the paper at the left side, near the upper edge, three fingers in front, with forefinger and thumb behind. As the glass comes in back of the paper, with the faces of the cards *toward you,* your left thumb and forefinger perform a secret action.

They draw the real four of hearts from the glass, leaving only the ten of diamonds. This is back toward the spectators. The right hand immediately sets the glass on the table while the left hand moves aside, carrying the paper. Since the spectators see a card in the glass, they naturally suppose that it is still the four of hearts.

Meanwhile, the left forefinger draws away, letting the thumb press the hidden four of hearts against the back of the paper. Holding the paper as though it was of no importance, you use the right hand to point from one glass to the other. You command the cards to pass.

With your right hand, you lift the cylinder from the covered glass. The spectators see the *four of hearts*. You remove it from the glass. Keeping it face toward the spectators, you place it beneath the fingers of the left hand, which press it against the front of the odd piece of paper.

Point to the glass that contains the reversed card; make the gesture with your right hand. Reach for the glass with the same hand and turn the tumbler around. In the glass, the audience sees the ten of diamonds.

As you lift the glass with your right hand, drop your left hand to your side and turn your body so that your right hand is toward the audience. This lets you swing your left hand so that the thumb side of the paper is toward the audience. Hand the glass to some one so that he can remove the ten of diamonds, then take the four of hearts from in front of the paper and give it to another party. The card that you take from the paper is the real four of hearts.

The crumpled paper cylinder is lying on the table; you can also have a few other sheets of paper if you wish. Lay down the paper that you hold in the left hand, placing it upon another sheet. Later, you can pick up two or three together, carrying the fake card between them.

PRESENTATION

The important features of this trick are the natural procedures that cover the vital moves. While various phases are important, two are especially so. One, when you steal away the front card from the glass; the other, when you substitute the fake card for the real four of hearts.

Note that the trick is particularly designed to mislead the spectators. Since you cover one glass, they are not looking for trickery when you state that you will merely turn the other about.

Nor will they suspect that the first card to change is a double faced one, because you have subtly shown the back of the other card, thus giving the impression that both are ordinary. They have forgotten the four of hearts when they see the ten of diamonds; hence no one will look for the belated exchange by the left hand. The passing out of the real four of hearts seems a most natural conclusion.

Work this trick in back of a table, or between two small tables. Have a glass at your right; place the two cards in it; and let the four of hearts face the audience.

For the next move: go to the glass on the left. Put the fake ten spot in it. Cover the glass with the improvised paper cylinder and make the turn around. Have papers on this table, and pick a small one to carry to the right. When you find the paper will not fit, stand with your left side to the audience and pick up the glass with your right hand.

Have the paper in your left hand, almost on the level of the glass, as if you intended to make another attempt at forming a cylinder. Half doubtful, you turn the glass so the back of the cards are toward the audience. You do this by a body move, facing the audience.

Your left hand remains stationary, which brings the glass in back of it. As you take the four of hearts, swing the glass downward and to the right, to place it on the table. Let the left hand drop to your left hip.

Stepping sideways, uncover the glass at the left, with the right hand. Remove the card; show it; and place it in front of the paper. Side-step to the glass on the right; turn it around with your right hand and show the ten of diamonds. Swing right hand and head to the right, as you raise the glass; then swing to the left. This lets your left hand make its half turn while covered by the body. From then on, keep the left hand with its thumb toward the audience.

Advance to the spectators. Give them the glass with the ten of diamonds in it. Reach for the four of hearts with the right hand; draw it from beneath the left thumb. Give it for examination; step back to the table and lay the paper, with fake card beneath it, on the sheets that are resting there.

The double-faced card needed for this trick will be found printed on a cardboard insert in this volume. One side shows the ten of diamonds, the other the four of hearts. The card, when cut out, will be the proper size for a standard pack of playing cards.

The Fifth Card

This card trick is of a special type in which the performer must concentrate upon an individual member of the audience. That point should be remembered. When performing before a group, one isolated member should be called upon for cooperation.

THE EFFECT

The magician shows five cards in a fan. He asks some one to concentrate upon a single card; to think of that card only and repeat its name to himself. The magician places the five cards in his pocket.

That done, he asks the person to write the name of the card upon a piece of paper; to fold the paper and place it on the table. One by one, the magician draws four cards from his pocket and lays them faces down beside the paper.

The magician states that he has retained the chosen card. The paper is unfolded; the name "Nine of Spades" is seen upon it. The spectator turns the four cards faces up; onlookers recognize them as the fanned cards, but the nine of spades is not among them.

From his pocket, the magician produces the chosen card. He has apparently read the spectator's thoughts, and the written paper bears such testimony.

THE METHOD

The cards in the fan, reading from left to right are: Six of Spades, Eight of Clubs, Nine of Spades, Five of Clubs, Seven of Spades. Previously placed in your pocket are four other cards; Five of Spades, Seven of Clubs, Eight of Spades, Nine of Clubs.

When a person has thought of one of the fanned cards, you turn them toward yourself. While he writes the name of his card, you arrange the fanned cards in order of value: Five, Six, Seven, Eight, Nine. Place them in your pocket, *beneath* the extra cards that you already have there.

When the paper is folded, bring out the extra cards and lay them in a row, faces down. The paper is unfolded after you state that you have retained the selected card. When the cards are turned up, spectators see cards so similar to the originals that they do not know they are viewing a new group.

Meanwhile, you have learned the selected card. Reach in your pocket; you calmly count the cards: Five, Six, Seven— until you reach the right one. Bring it out to show that it corresponds to the name on the piece of paper.

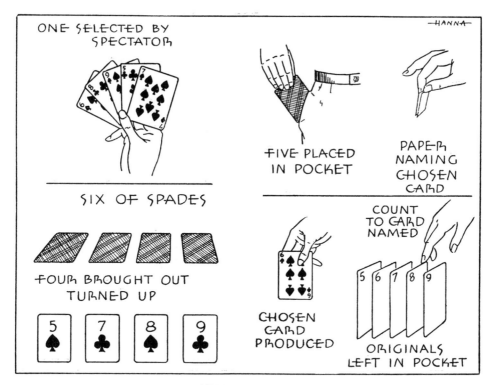

ONE SELECTED BY
SPECTATOR

—HANNA—

FIVE PLACED
IN POCKET

PAPER
NAMING
CHOSEN
CARD

SIX OF SPADES

FOUR BROUGHT OUT
TURNED UP

COUNT
TO CARD
NAMED

5 6 7 8 9

5♠ 7♣ 8♠ 9♣

CHOSEN
CARD
PRODUCED

ORIGINALS
LEFT IN POCKET

PRESENTATION

Presentation is important in this trick because you have a subtle task to handle. You must make people think that they see the same cards twice; therefore, you must neither give them too long a glimpse nor too brief a view.

As a "one man" trick, concentrating upon a lone spectator, the task is simple. You merely show him the fan; ask him to concentrate upon one card and retain that lone thought. He is so busy remembering the one card that he can not try to remember the others; particularly if you do not give him too long to choose.

As for other spectators, they must be properly convinced. To produce the right effect on them, have your lone "subject" away from the rest of the group. Show the fanned cards; display them to the spectators, but not to the man who is to make the choice. Remark that you have a fan of five cards.

Do not state what you intend to do; and keep your hand moving slowly while you let the spectators view them. Turn to your "subject" and concentrate upon him; from that point onward, no one else sees the faces of the cards.

Having gained a general impression of five black spot cards, the spectators will naturally take the four extras to be originals. It is a bold bluff, this exchange of cards that have been shown to the audience; but it is psychologically sound and therefore succeeds.

As the extra cards are turned up on the table, you can subtly remark: "There is one that you saw; but not the one you chose—"; "There is the Six of Spades; for a moment you were on the point of selecting it—"; or any other appropriate remark. Such points of emphasis add to the deception.

The trick may be performed with red cards instead of blacks. In that case, fan the following: Six of Hearts, Eight of Diamonds, Nine of Hearts, Five of Diamonds, Seven of Hearts. In your pocket, have the Five of Hearts, Seven of Diamonds, Eight of Hearts, Nine of Diamonds.

Basically, this trick depends upon a confusion that always exists in a person's mind between similar cards of different suits, particularly the seven and eight spots. The introduction of fives and nines of opposite suits makes it even more difficult for an observer to gain an exact impression of the cards.

A card of one value has to be absent from the second group; the Six serves that purpose admirably, for its figure is so similar to that of the Nine. At the finish, when the selected card is brought from the pocket, people may see a Six and a Nine; two Sixes or two Nines; but never three of those values.

In picking the selected card from the pocket, the blind counting can be done easily and deliberately, for attention will be centered on the cards that are being turned up on the table. Should the paper name the card as a Five, Six, or Seven, count down to the right card. For an Eight or a Nine, you can either count down, or count up in reverse: Nine—Eight.

The chosen card should be drawn from the pocket in a careless fashion as though you merely reached in and plucked forth the only card there.

ORIENTAL MAGIC

People talk about the feats of Oriental wonder-workers: the Hindu fakirs and the Chinese wizards. Since they talk about such tricks, they like to see them.

This section consists entirely of tricks that have been adapted from those of Oriental magicians. They have been chosen because of their simplicity and their effectiveness.

The simplest tricks are always the best when properly presented. You will learn that fact yourself when you practice this Magic of the East. The tricks are suitable in any program. There are also enough in this section to give a complete program of Oriental Magic.

TRICKS IN THIS SECTION

The Magnetic Chop-Stick

The Levitated Tube

The Rope and the Vase

String and Scissors

The Chinese Joss Cards

The Burmese Wand

The Magnetic Chop-Stick

This is an excellent trick to use as an opening in a routine of Oriental Magic. With rice and chop-stick as the items used, it has a real Chinese flavor.

THE EFFECT

A bottle is filled with rice. The magician takes a chop-stick and presses it down through the neck of the bottle, deep into the rice. He says a few Chinese words and lifts the end of the chop-stick. The bottle load of rice comes up from the table.

THE METHOD

Simply press the chop-stick firmly. The rice will do the rest. The pressure of the stick forces rice to the sides of the bottle. Wedged in a mass, the grains choke the bottle neck and the rice grips the chop-stick firmly.

To release the chop-stick, hold the bottle in the left hand and twist the chop-stick with the right. The stick will come out easily.

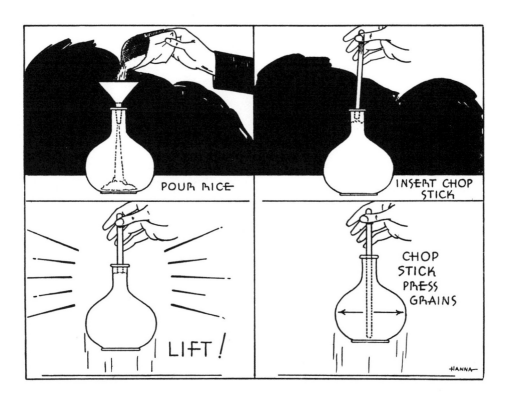

POUR RICE

INSERT CHOP STICK

LIFT!

CHOP STICK PRESS GRAINS

HANNA

PRESENTATION

A transparent bottle is preferable, as the rice can then be seen inside it. A rounded bottle, or any of an unusual shape naturally looks better than an ordinary medicine bottle; therefore an odd bottle should be used, if obtainable.

The following patter is suitable:

"Everything goes backwards in China; hence the Chinese have unusual methods of performing ordinary actions. Let me demonstrate how they carry a bottle of rice.

"First they fill the bottle with rice; that part is ordinary enough, as there is no way around it. But does the Chinaman pick up the bottle and place it in his hand? Not a bit of it; he wants a handle for the bottle, so he takes the first object that he thinks of, which happens to be a chop-stick.

"He pushes the chop-stick down into the rice. He talks to the bottle nicely, in Chinese." *Repeat a few words of pretended Chinese.* "The rice always responds to such talk. When the Chinaman picks up the chop-stick, the bottle comes with it.

"Its owner can carry the bottle anywhere, as long as he wants. When he needs the handle no longer, he simply removes the chop-stick."

Pour the rice into a bowl, after the trick. If a chop-stick is not obtainable, an unsharpened pencil of hexagonal shape will serve instead.

The Levitated Tube

In its original form, this Hindu trick was performed with a special tube and a single piece of cord. The present adaptation requires simpler items: an ordinary sheet of paper of about typewriter size; two pieces of light twine, each a little more than a yard in length; and a pair of paper fasteners to hold the paper when rolled into the form of a tube. With these inexpensive props, the Hindu miracle can be outdone.

THE EFFECT

The magician shows a long, thin paper tube, held by pointed fasteners with spread-out ends. Two lengths of thin twine run through the tube. The magician draws them back and forth. He finally takes two ends of the strings in one hand; two ends in the other hand. He lets the tube slide down along the strings.

At the magician's command, the tube stops. It slides again when he orders it to do so. When the tube has neared the bottom of the strings, the magician tells it to rise. The tube obeys, ascending the string slowly and steadily, stopping only when he commands it.

This surprising demonstration is repeated several times. Sliding the tube about midway on the strings, the magician takes a string from each end of the tube and ties them. A spectator holds these ends. The magician ties the other two ends; gives them to another spectator. Both persons pull; the tube comes away from the strings. The paper fasteners are removed. The tube is shown to be an ordinary sheet of paper.

THE METHOD

The tube is exactly what it appears to be; a rolled sheet of paper. It is rolled while upright, to make it as long as possible. The tube should be about an inch in diameter. In fastening the tube, it is important to push the fasteners from the inside, outward. Thus the heads of the metal fasteners are within the tube; the points are spread on the outside surface.

Take one piece of string; double it. Insert the looped center into the tube and hook it over the head of the fastener. Let the string hang full length from the tube.

Place the second string *beneath* the doubled one. Raise the ends of the second string and bring them together so that it is doubled also. Push the ends of this string all the way through the tube. When they come out the other end, pull them.

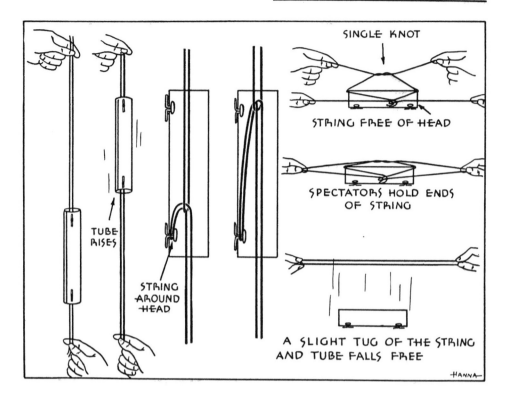

This is the *upper* end of the tube. You will find that the ends of the second string draw the first string upward. You can then pull the strings back and forth from either end. The doubled strings appear to be two separate ones that run straight through the tube.

When ready to demonstrate, draw the upper strings almost to the top of the tube; then pull the lower strings clear down to the head of the paper fastener, thus proving that the supposedly single strings run freely through the tube.

Take the upper strings with one hand; the lower with the other. Hold the tube upright. Friction of the strings will hold it there; but slight shakes of the upper hand will cause it to descend.

When the tube has descended to its limit pull both ends of the strings. Watch the tube; not your hands. The tube will ascend the strings in mysterious fashion. Though your hands lengthen the strings, the fact is not noticeable. When the tube has gone as high as it will travel, shake it down again. Cause it to make another climb.

After several repetitions of this mystery, tilt the tube to horizontal position. Let some one hold the tube while you draw the strings midway. Take a string from each end; tie them in a single knot. Have a person hold them.

Take the two remaining strings; tie them in a single knot and give them to the person who holds the tube. You receive the tube and begin to adjust it. This action enables you to slip your forefinger into the lower end of the tube. There you slide the loop of the lower string free from the paper fastener.

Tell the persons to pull the ends of the strings. They do so; at the same time, you raise the tube and edge the persons further apart. The strings come clear; each person is holding the ends of two taut strings. The tube has apparently passed through the strings themselves.

PRESENTATION

You can have the tube made up at the start of the trick and you can show it quite freely. With light twine and a tube of small diameter, there is no chance of any one seeing the peculiar looping of the strings.

At the finish, unfasten the paper; give it for examination. Its innocent appearance puzzles the spectators, particularly when they find no unusual appliance. They never suspect that the paper fasteners were necessary to the trick.

The following patter makes a good story for this trick:

"In India, the fakirs perform feats of self-levitation, floating in mid-air whenever they so choose. I shall not attempt to rise in the air; it is dangerous in a room with a low ceiling, because it is difficult to gauge one's limit. I shall, however, demonstrate a Hindu experiment in levitation.

"Observe this paper tube with strings that pass through it. The strings are useful because they serve as a measure of the distance that the tube can move. The strings run back and forth until I tilt the tube. Then they run up and down.

"The tube, naturally, slides down. Watch it stop. Now it slides again. Quite a neat trick, making the tube obey. But it is more wonderful when the tube reverses the process. Here comes the levitation. I command the tube to rise.

"Up it goes. Stop! Up again—up—up—that's far enough. Slide down. Stop. Slide again. Rise! Once more the tube rivals the celebrated fakirs who lift themselves in the air."

Repeat the fall and rise a few times. Then prepare for the final effect.

"The Hindus have another puzzling problem involving a tube and cords. Suppose I demonstrate it. First some one must hold the tube. Next, I tie the ends of two strings. Will you hold them please?

"Now the other ends. Here they are, for you to hold. Let me have the tube while you take care of the strings. You crumpled the tube a bit; that will not matter. I can straighten it. There it is, as good as ever.

"Pull. Slowly—at both ends. The Hindu charm works. The tube is free. You have the cords. Quite a remarkable tube to free itself without damage. Yet the tube is nothing but a piece of paper. I shall unroll it for you.

"No need to worry about the tube and the strings. They are just what they appear to be. The real secret depends upon my knowledge of the Hindu system, which makes everything ordinary become extraordinary."

The Rope and the Vase

More elaborate than the "Magnetic Chop-Stick," this trick allows a complete routine in its performance. It is a feat of genuine Chinese Magic, long performed in the Orient.

THE EFFECT

The magician shows a rounded vase; a two foot length of thin rope. He inserts the end of the rope in the vase and winds the rest of the rope about the neck.

Inverting the vase, the magician lets the rope dangle downward. Oddly, it does not drop from the vase; but hangs suspended there. Lifting the hanging end of the rope, the magician lowers the vase. This time, the mystery is reversed. The vase hangs, unsupported, from the rope.

The magician commands the vase to swing back and forth. It does so. He orders it to stop; it stands still. Next, at his command, the vase begins to swing in a large circle. Finally, he grasps the vase and removes the rope.

Both items may then be examined by the spectators, with no clue to the mystery.

THE METHOD

Inside the vase is a little rubber ball. Its diameter, plus that of the rope, must be a little greater than the width of the vase neck.

In winding the rope about the neck of the vase, tilt the vase mouth downward. The ball will slide into the neck. A slight tightening of the rope will grip the ball in place.

The rope will then hang when the vase is inverted. Conversely, the vase will cling to the rope. The final effect, the swinging of the vase, is accomplished by an unnoticeable motion of the hand that holds the rope.

Simply let the vase dangle at full length of the rope. When you want it to swing in pendulum fashion, your hand will respond; although you do not have to move it purposely. Similarly, when you want the vase to stop, you will find that your muscles will tighten.

You can make it swing in a circle, through the same subconscious impulse. To conclude the trick, grip the vase by the neck with your left hand. Hold the neck between your thumb and forefinger, with the left hand cupped palm upward below the mouth of the vase.

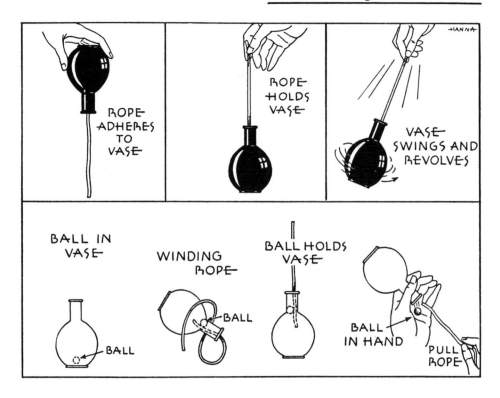

Pull out the rope with the right hand. A steady draw will remove the rope and the ball will drop unnoticed into the left hand.

PRESENTATION

The ball is in the vase at the start; unless you prefer to allow a preliminary examination of the vase and rope. In that case, you must have the ball between the thumb and fingers of your hand; in receiving the vase, take it at the mouth and let the ball drop into the vase.

When you insert the rope, allow a good length into the vase; as you wind the rope, draw slightly when you tilt the vase at an angle, mouth downward. Resistance will tell when the ball catches.

If the ball fails to catch, let the vase twist as you wind the rope. If the ball fails to enter the neck at all, unwind the rope and begin over again. The ball usually finds its place on the first attempt.

Your patter can take care of this. There is no need for speed with the trick. The outline given here will serve as a guide to suitable patter.

"This is a Chinese temple vase, used for purposes of divination. In order to put the vase to its test, we require a piece of rope; this one is quite suitable.

"The Chinaman inserts the rope in the vase; then winds the rope around the vase to create a magnetic current. He must be very careful with the winding; any unevenness will prevent the magnetic result.

"Having wound the rope successfully, the patient Chinaman gives it the test. He holds the vase upside down; the rope hangs from it, but does not fall. Wonderful? Not at all. Watch what comes next.

"I hold the end of the rope. The vase hangs this time. It is now ready to give the answer to any question that concerns the future. I think of a question. I watch the vase.

"Look. It swings back and forth. That is too bad; it means that the wish will not come true. Stop! That's enough. Now for another question. Ah! This time it is better. The vase circles. That means that the wish will be granted. That is, my second wish, but not the first one. The vase is never wrong.

"The Chinese never annoy the vase after it has given an affirmative answer to one wish. Instead, they remove the rope and put the vase back on its shelf until the next time it is needed.

"You would like to see the vase? Certainly. Here it is; and the rope, too. Try it for yourself; but remember to dangle the rope first. If you can't make the rope hang, the vase won't. You can't do it? That is probably because the vase has already granted its daily wish.

"Rarely, if ever, does the vase respond after it has given one affirmative answer. Its motto is like that of the Chinese boy scouts: 'Always put off a good deed until to-morrow if you have already done one to-day'."

String and Scissors

This is a modification of a trick with ropes and rings. Using scissors and a length of cord, the feat may be performed at closer range.

THE EFFECT

The magician introduces a pair of scissors, a long pencil and a twelve inch length of string. He ties both handles of the scissors to the pencil.

A pull of the pencil; a tug of the string. The scissors come free.

THE METHOD

Have the person hold the scissors upside down in closed position. Tie the cord around the center of the pencil. Push both ends of the string through one handle of the scissors; separate the ends and bring them back around the pencil for another knot.

Push the ends of the string through the other handle of the scissors; again spread them and bring them back around the pencil. Tie the final knot, as many times as you wish.

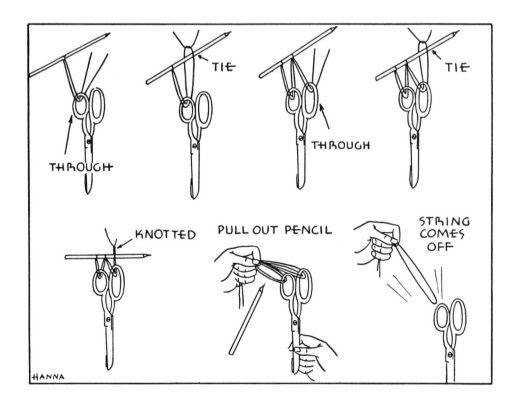

Simply close your hand around the center of the string; draw the pencil out of the knots that gird it. Pull the ends of the string; if the center hangs to the scissors, spread it with the hand that covers. The scissors are held by loops only; they will come free.

PRESENTATION

Present the trick as an experiment in Chinese rope tying. The following patter will fit well with the routine.

"In China, the river boatmen are very thorough in their methods of mooring their boats. Every sampan has a ring attached to its bow; so has the wharf where the boat is tied. The handles of these scissors represent the rings.

"Since the current in the Yangtze Kiang, otherwise the Yellow River, is very strong, the boatman first ties his rope to a spike represented by this pencil. Then he ties it to the ring on the sampan and then around the spike again. He ties the rope to the ring on the wharf and makes the job thorough by finally tying it around the spike.

"When flood waters come down the Yangtze, the sampan owner offsets the strain by removing the spike. That gives the rope proper slack, so that the boat will not be buried beneath the water. But somehow, the old Chinese river has its own way of handling tricky knots.

"One tug of those yellow waters; away come the ropes; and that's the end of the Chinese sampan."

The Chinese Joss Cards

The Chinese Joss Cards are an adaptation of an Oriental mystery in which a cord is cut and restored. While especially appropriate for a program of Oriental Magic, it may be utilized in other types of routine.

THE EFFECT

The magician has several cards that are embellished with Chinese characters. These have holes punched near the ends. Ribbons run through each end, so that the cards form the rungs of a miniature ladder.

The cards are drawn back and forth along the ribbons. Each ribbon is pulled separately in one direction; then in the other. The magician states that he will use either ribbon in the trick; so he asks the spectators to choose one.

With one ribbon selected, the magician winds the other about the ends of the cards and ties it in place. He holds the loose ribbon upward and draws it back and forth. Spreading the loose ends of the cards, he shows the ribbon between the cards and asks the spectators to cut it with a pair of scissors.

That done, the magician announces that the joss cards will manifest a curious restoration. After a few moments, he pulls one end of the loose ribbon. It runs through the cards just as it did before. The cut ribbon is restored.

To conclude this demonstration, the magician lets a person take the short end of the restored ribbon. The magician walks away with the cards; the ribbon comes completely clear. It is then in the hands of the spectators who can examine it and see that the restoration is complete.

THE METHOD

Nine cards are used and they conceal a peculiar arrangement of the ribbons. To prepare the trick, thread the ribbons through the cards. Hold the cards flat and turn the top card end around. Turn the pack over and do the same with the card that was originally the bottom one of the stack.

The ribbons are thus criss-crossed beneath each end card. This can not be seen, since the cards are held in a stack. When you pull one ribbon back and forth, it appears to run straight through the cards. The same is the case with the other ribbon.

It makes no difference which ribbon is chosen. Simply wind the other around its end of the cards to keep it in place; but do not tie it too tightly, as you want a little play between the cards.

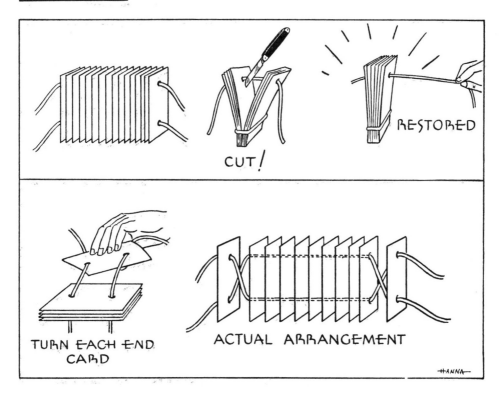

CUT!

RESTORED

TURN EACH END CARD

ACTUAL ARRANGEMENT

—HANNA—

Hold the loose end of the cards upward; pull the chosen ribbon back and forth a few times more and finally center it. Then spread the cards near the middle, and invite some one to cut the ribbon.

The spectator thinks that he is cutting the loose ribbon. Actually, he is cutting the center of the lower ribbon. After the cut, you have merely to draw the loose ribbon back and forth. It will run as freely as before.

When some one takes the end of the loose ribbon, you can walk away and the ribbon will run free from the cards. That leaves the restored ribbon in the hands of the spectators.

NOTATIONS

While the trick is effective with the criss-cross arrangement made beforehand, it is possible to actually thread the ribbons through the cards in the presence of the spectators. If this is done, you must turn the top card and the bottom one after the trick has begun.

The best way is to hold the cards in the left hand; thumb at one side, fingers at the other. Lift the top card with the right hand, thumb at the near end, fingers at the far end. Twist the left hand to the left, the right hand to the right, in rotary fashion, turning the cards over at the same time.

The back of the right hand should be kept toward the audience, thus covering the manoeuver. Repeat the action, thus reversing the card at the other end of the stack. The movement appears to be a mere adjustment of the cards, as if you were squaring them to bring the holes in line. You can also mask these moves by walking from one group of persons to another; or by stepping to a table to obtain a pair of scissors.

After the ribbon has been restored and drawn from the cards, the simplest process is to pocket the cards, or lay them aside. You can, however, add a neat aftermath. As the ribbon comes clear, tighten the ribbon which is tied about the lower ends of the cards. This will draw the cut portions of the ribbon from the upper holes. You may then riffle the upper ends of the cards, to show the holes from which the restored ribbon supposedly came. When you take back the ribbon from the spectators, you can calmly thread it through the upper holes and pull it back and forth a few times before you lay the cards aside.

PRESENTATION

The presentation is given in its simplest form, with appropriate patter. The individual performer can add any necessary remarks to cover variations or additions in routine.

"These are Chinese Joss Cards, that are supposed to possess remarkable powers. Each card has a different significance, according to the character inscribed upon it.

"These sets of cards hang like little ladders in the Chinese temples." *Spread the cards slightly along the ribbons.* "They are always kept together as their power would be lost if they were separated or their proper order disturbed."

Start to draw one ribbon through the cards; then the other.

"A peculiar charm protects these Joss Cards. To demonstrate it, I shall ask you to choose one ribbon. This one? Good. Since the other is no longer needed, I shall tie it around its end of the cards."

Wind the lower ribbon; twist its ends and knot them. A spectator can tie the knot if you wish; if he does, hold the cards tightly during the process.

"We shall draw the chosen ribbon back and forth through the ladder of cards until we find the exact center. Here it is, somewhere among the cards. Just spread those cards at the middle. You see the ribbon? Cut it with the scissors.

"If it were not for the power of the Joss Cards, the ends would fall apart if I released them. But the Joss Cards prefer to stay together. Please preserve silence while I repeat the mystic characters that are printed on the cards."

Hold the cards in your left hand. Raise the right forefinger and mumble pretended words in Chinese.

"The charm is completed. The cards are still joined. Look! The ribbon is restored; it runs back and forth as it did before. . . . What? You would like to see the ribbon more closely? Very well. Since the cards are tied at one end, I can risk removing the restored ribbon. Take the short end. Hold it tight, while I draw the cards from it.

"There you have the ribbon, as good as ever, despite the fact that you clipped it. That proves that the Chinese Joss Cards still retain their power even when removed from the temple where they belong."

If you decide to replace the ribbon, push it through the cards and wrap it around the ends, with the added remarks:

"In order that the Joss Cards will retain their mystic force, I must replace the ribbon and wrap it around them. Such was the instruction of the Chinese wizard who brought them from the temple in Hankow."

The cards necessary for this trick will be found among the cardboard inserts in this volume. Cut them apart along the separating lines.

Each card is marked with the necessary holes. These can be pierced with a large needle, and the trick performed with lengths of thin string. If ribbons are preferred, the holes should be made with a punch.

Strings or ribbons should be about two feet in length. If ribbons are employed, be sure to obtain narrow ones, no wider than the holes.

The Burmese Wand

This is an excellent finish to a routine of Oriental Magic. The trick can be performed either with or without an assistant; but the latter course is preferable.

THE EFFECT

The magician shows a rounded stick, which he terms a Burmese wand. He winds a cord around the stick while the ends are held by an assistant. To the ends of the cord, the magician attaches a heavy object.

At the magician's command, the suspended object drops to the floor, carrying the cords with it. The cords have passed through the solid wand, although the ends of the stick have been held all the while.

THE METHOD

Have a very short pin or a small tack pressed in the center of the wand. This side should be kept from view. Take a string and lay it across the wand, so that both ends dangle, the longer end in front.

Catch the front end of the cord and wind it three times around the wand, drawing it under toward the back, then over toward the front. Wind it toward the center of the wand and keep it *between* the loose end of the cord and the center pin.

When you come over the top on the third turn, carry the cord in front of the pin. Then wind down in back, up in front, for three more turns. These are on the *far side* of the pin. When you come down with the last turn, take both ends of the cord and tie them to an object such as a metal ring and let it dangle.

Your assistant then revolves the wand slowly between his hands, so that the cords unwind. When they have gone the right distance, they slip from the pin. The cords drop from the wand.

You can wind the wand yourself and hold the ends if you choose. With a loose pin, the cords will snap loose as you come to the final turn, carrying the pin with them.

PRESENTATION

While a wand is best for this trick, a walking stick, a piece of dowel, or a chair rung will serve the purpose. Any attachable object will do for the weight: a metal ring, a dinner bell, or a gong. The gong is preferable, as it has an Oriental appearance. A dark stick is best, with a black pin or tack as it can be shown at closer range. Fancy cords look better than ordinary string.

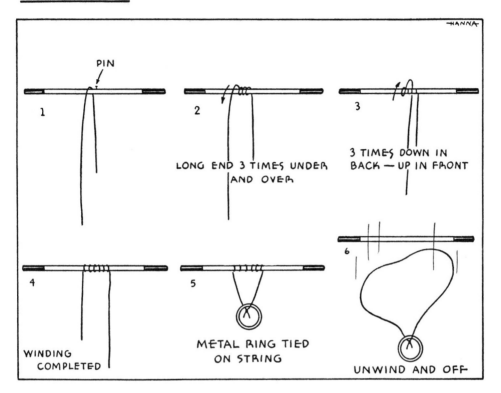

The following patter is effective with this trick:

"In the famous Burmese temple described by Kipling, there hangs a mysterious wand. It is girded with a heavy cord, in this fashion. From its ends are suspended a sacred gong.

"Only the initiated are allowed to strike that gong. Should a stranger enter the temple and attempt the task himself, the gong would immediately express its disapproval.

"Here we have the wand; a solid stick of wood with cords around it. The ends of the wand are held; the gong hangs below. Watch and you will see the mystery of the Burmese temple.

"One false approach by an invader; the wand no longer keeps the gong suspended. It drops to the temple floor—like that. Yet the wand is as solid as ever. The cord? Here it is, still firmly tied and tightly attached to the sacred gong."

MENTAL MAGIC

Strange feats of divination; mental mysteries that baffle explanation—such are the type of tricks that comprise this section.

You will find that such tricks impress your audience more than any other type of magic; yet these are often the easiest to perform.

Most of them depend upon simple but well concealed systems, which are easily learned but difficult to detect. That is why they are always popular when shown as a form of entertainment.

You can form a complete program of mental mysteries from the material offered in this section. Some of the tricks which appear similar are actually quite different when you know the secrets.

Hence, you can vary your methods, using one trick to strengthen another and carrying your audiences further from the solutions upon which these mental mysteries depend.

TRICKS IN THIS SECTION

The Mystic Disks

Match Pack Divination

Four Safety Pins

The Detective Mystery

The New Magic Square

The Mystic Alphabet

The Mystic Disks

This trick is one of color divination, whereby the magician apparently detects the color of an object by employing the sense of touch.

THE EFFECT

The magician uses three cardboard disks, each of the same size but of a different color. One disk is red; one is green; one is white. The disks are passed for inspection.

The magician turns away from the spectators and places his hand behind his back. He asks that one of the disks be placed in his hand; that the others be hidden elsewhere. When this is done, the magician faces the spectators, still holding the disk behind him.

Soon, the magician names the color of the disk. His statement is correct. He repeats the trick a few times, to prove that his color touch is always accurate.

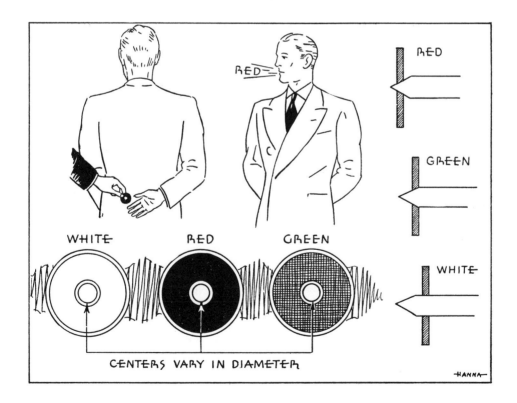

THE METHOD

Each disk has a small hole in the center. Though the disks are equal in diameter, the holes are not. They vary by a tiny fraction of an inch.

This difference is not enough for the spectators to notice. Should they suspect the variation, they will not see how it could aid the performer. Nevertheless, it is because of that difference that the trick can be accomplished.

In addition to the disks, you must carry a short lead pencil. This can be hidden in one hand; or you can have it up your sleeve, or in your hip pocket. When you face the spectators, obtain the pencil and slide its point into the hole in the disk that you hold.

The red disk should have the smallest center; the pencil tip will enter it only half way. The green disk has the center next in size; the pencil tip will just push to the top of its taper. The white disk, with a slightly larger hole, will slip over the pencil.

PRESENTATION

Talk to the spectators when you face them; state that you are actually feeling for the color of the disk. That statement covers your motions with the pencil. After you name the color, ask if it is correct; while you are receiving an answer, you can dispose of the pencil. Then give the disk to the spectators with your other hand.

Repetition is valuable in this trick, as only three objects are used, hence one guess could be sheer luck. Let one hand idle at your side, between each repetition, keeping the pencil in readiness. No one has reason to suppose that you are using an extra object in the trick.

At the finish, ask for the disks as though you intend to repeat the trick. Instead, simply put them in your pocket. If you have not already disposed of the pencil in your hip pocket, you can put it away with the disks.

Use a pencil with a broken point, so that the disks will not become accidentally marked.

> Disks suitable for this trick are printed on one of the cardboard inserts in this volume. They can be cut out and used as the necessary apparatus.

Match Pack Divination

This is one of the best of divination tricks, as it is performed with borrowed objects. The items used are match packs. Since they are always available, the trick can be presented in any type of program.

THE EFFECT

The magician shows some packs of paper matches, each of a different pattern. He lays them on the table; asks some one to choose any match pack and open it while the magician's back is turned. The person can remove a match if he wishes; whether he does or not, he is to close the pack and replace it with the others. They are then handed to the magician.

Holding each pack to his forehead, one by one, the magician finally selects one and tosses it on the table. The pack that the magician picks is the one that the spectators chose.

THE METHOD

You take each pack that you intend to use and open it, to show the matches inside. When you close the pack, press its

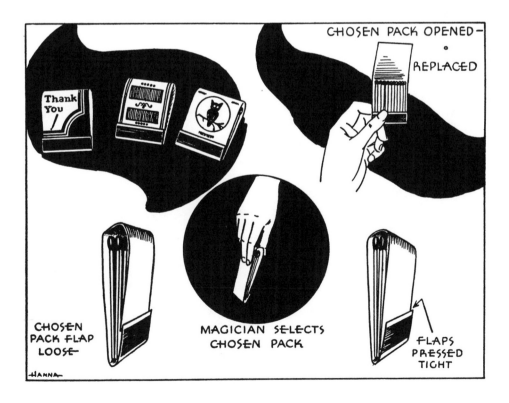

cover firmly with your thumb, thus wedging the loose flap tightly shut. This slight action is not noticeable as you keep your thumb away from view.

When a person opens the selected match pack, he unwittingly loosens the tight flap. Closing the pack in normal fashion, he fails to wedge the flap like the others. When you receive the packs and hold them to your forehead, you keep the flap sides toward you and test them with pressure of your thumb. The one that opens without pressure is the chosen one.

PRESENTATION

Present this trick simply as a feat of divination, borrowing match packs for the purpose. Have a few packs of your own; showing the matches in them, as with the others. Then proceed with the effect.

In showing the matches, you tighten the flaps; and thus note any packs that happen to be too loose. Reject those, either stating that you have too many, or that there are not enough matches in those packs (which is usually the case with loose-flapped packets).

Be sure to have five or six packs of your own; all ones that wedge tightly. Toss them in with the borrowed lot; then show the packs singly. You will then be sure of having enough suitable packs for the trick.

Four Safety Pins

This divination feat requires some preparation; but the items used are of such ordinary appearance that the trick appears to lack any previous arrangement.

THE EFFECT

The magician shows four safety pins, all alike. The pins are clasped; each has a tiny bit of ribbon attached to it. The ribbons are of different colors.

One of these pins is given to the magician, behind his back. He immediately names the color of its ribbon.

THE METHOD

First, dull the points of two safety pins with a file or by rubbing them against a stone. Then attach the ribbons to each pin, according to the following arrangement:

(1)   Red ribbon. On solid bar of a dull pin.
(2)   White ribbon. On solid bar of a sharp pin.
(3)   Green ribbon. On loose bar of a dull pin.
(4)   Blue ribbon. On loose bar of a sharp pin.

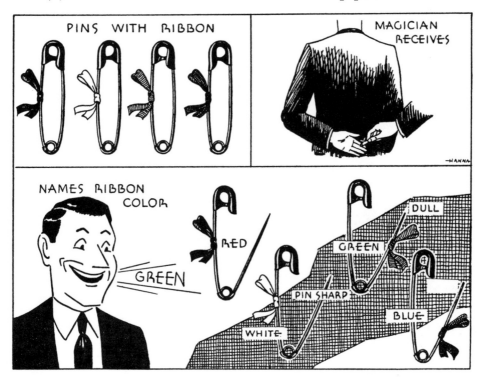

To learn the color of any ribbon, simply open the pin and find whether its point is sharp or dull. Note also if the ribbon is tied to the loose bar or the solid. These two clues give you the color of the ribbon.

PRESENTATION

Show the pins closed; call attention to the fact that they are all alike. Open each and clasp it again; no one will notice the difference in the points. Nor will they see the location of the ribbons, as your fingers cover them.

This makes all seem fair. Point to the ribbons; show that they differ in color only, hence they can furnish no clues. Ask some one to pocket the pins; then bring one out after you have turned your back.

Receive the safety pin with one hand behind you. Face the spectators and open the pin behind your back. Learn the color of the ribbon; close the pin as you name the color.

Ask for the other pins; give them to another person and repeat the trick. When you receive the pins from the second spectator, do not repeat the divination. Either lay the safety pins aside or place them in your pocket.

Since persons do not know that you intend to finish the trick so soon, they will have no opportunity to give the pins a further examination.

The Detective Mystery

This is a memory feat that will impress any audience. It can be used in a program of mental magic, or it may be introduced as a separate feat of its own. People who witness it usually credit the performer with being a memory expert.

THE EFFECT

The performer introduces two sets of cards. Two dozen compose a set; one group has the names of articles, printed in red; the other set has names of places, in green. Each card displays a different statement.

Announcing that he will demonstrate the memory skill that is required of a detective, the performer asks some one to shuffle the two sets separately; then deal him two cards at a time, one from each group.

Receiving a pair of cards, the performer reads them and gives them to a spectator, saying: "The red card is the clue; the green card is the scene. Please hold these cards until later."

He does this with the next pair of cards, giving them to another spectator; and he continues thus until all the cards have been paired and distributed.

The performer then requests: "Read me the name of an object listed on a red card. Ask me where the detective found that clue."

Some one questions: "Where did the detective find the knife?" To which the performer replies: "In the lake."

The spectator reads the question from the red card. Looking at the green card that he holds with it, he finds that the performer has given the answer printed on the green card. Another question is put by the spectator: "Where did the detective find the false teeth?" The performer answers: "In the garage." He is right again.

As fast as the remaining red cards are called, the performer gives the answers on the green cards, pairing them correctly every time, just as they were dealt from the shuffled heaps. With apparently no effort, he has memorized two dozen pairs of objects.

THE METHOD

This is not a test of memory; it is simply a matter of associating ideas. The clues on the red cards are all objects which can be easily pictured mentally. Similarly, the places named in green can be visualized with little effort.

Every time you take a pair of cards, half-close your eyes and picture the red object in the green place. It is easy to think of a knife at the bottom of a lake, with some one fishing for it. Similarly, false teeth attached to the steering wheel of an automobile, are easily remembered.

Many of the possible pairs are incongruous, which makes them all the more easily remembered. A gorilla in an ice box, for example; finger prints in a tree; a policeman in a water tower.

Concentrate upon each pair until you have the mental picture; then give the cards to a spectator. Say nothing to him about picturing the situation. Just ask him to hold the cards for future reference.

Go right on with the next pair, concentrating to form your picture. Do not try to remember any of them. They will jump to mind the moment that people begin to read from the green cards. When they ask you where the detective found the gorilla, you will think of the ice box the moment you hear the question.

You can experiment with the trick, using less than the two dozen pairs; and can, of course, limit it to any number that suits you. When you come to present the trick on another occasion, you will find that your new concentration upon the pairs that are dealt will obliterate the associations that you used in the previous performance.

> The sets of cards for this trick are printed on sheets of cardboard and are bound with the inserts in this volume. Cut them along the dividing lines and you will have the required apparatus.

The New Magic Square

This is a puzzling mathematical effect. While it is dependent upon a numerical system, and can be done with a chart of ordinary figures, one with playing cards is preferable; as it tends to mislead the spectators.

THE EFFECT

Thirty-six cards are arranged in six rows. Each card is designated by its value. Ace, 1; two, 2; and so on. A Jack counts 11; a Queen, 12; a King, 13.

These cards are printed in miniature, upon a chart. The vertical rows bear designating letters: A, B, C, D, E and F. The arrangement of the rows is as follows:

(A)	(B)	(C)	(D)	(E)	(F)
Ace	2	3	4	5	6
2	3	4	5	6	7
3	4	5	6	7	8
6	7	8	9	10	Jack
7	8	9	10	Jack	Queen
8	9	10	Jack	Queen	King

A spectator is provided with six coins. He is told to place one coin on a card in the first cross-row; a coin on a card in the second cross-row; and so on. One coin for each horizontal row; but the coin may be placed on any card in its row.

The magician turns his back before the coins are placed. Still turned away, he asks the spectator to note the letters that mark the vertical rows; and to tell him how many coins are in each lettered row. For example: the spectator may announce that there are two coins in vertical row A; one in row B; none in rows C or D; two in row E; one in row F.

The spectator says nothing else. He gives no clue to where the coins lie in any row, either horizontal or vertical. Yet the magician immediately names a total. When the spectator counts the values of the cards that he has covered by coins, he finds that the magician's total was correct.

THE METHOD

The formula is quite simple. Give the coins values according to their lettered rows. Count every coin in row A as 4; in row B, 5; in row C, 6; in row D, 7, in row E, 8; in row F, 9. To that sum add 3, to make the final total.

In the example given, two coins in row A would count 8; one in row B, 5, making 13; two in row E, 16, making 29; one in row F, 9, making 38; plus 3, for a total of 41.

This will work every time, provided that the rule is followed: First, each of the six coins must be placed in a different cross-row. Second, you must be told how many coins are in each vertical, lettered row.

COMMENT

To explain the basic principle of this system, we have provided a simple example. Consider three rows as follows:

$$1 \quad 2 \quad 3$$
$$2 \quad 3 \quad 4$$
$$3 \quad 4 \quad 5$$

Note that the middle cross-line (2, 3, 4) provides the key. You can count any coin in the first vertical row as 2; any in the second as 3; any in the third as 4. The coin on the first cross-row will be valued one number too high; but that one point will be deducted from the coin on the lowest cross-row.

The Card Chart has been arranged so that it *has no key-line*. Its key-numbers are the mid-point between the third cross-row and the fourth. Hence the actual key-numbers are $4\frac{1}{2}$, $5\frac{1}{2}$, $6\frac{1}{2}$, $7\frac{1}{2}$, $8\frac{1}{2}$, $9\frac{1}{2}$. Since there are certain to be six halves, we simply use 4, 5, 6, 7, 8, 9 as key-numbers and add 3 at the finish.

This makes the chart deceptive; completely covers any clues that would occur to most persons. With six rows, the effect becomes quite puzzling and the trick may be repeated to baffle the spectators more than ever.

The card chart needed for this trick appears among the cardboard inserts of this volume. The cards are printed in miniature, so that they are about the size of coins, which makes the trick more workable. The vertical lines are designated by printed letters. The chart may be removed from the book and used for the trick.

Any time the chart is not available, the trick may be performed with a pack of cards. When a pack is used, lay out black cards along with the reds. Slips of paper can be marked to designate the lettered vertical rows.

The Mystic Alphabet

There have been numerous divination tricks in which spectators pick names or numbers that are printed on cards, then ask the performer to declare the chosen one. Invariably, the cards on which the selected item appears must be returned to the magician, who thereupon looks for a "key" word or number in order to announce the choice.

In the "Mystic Alphabet" a new principle has been introduced. The performer does not glimpse the faces of the cards after the trick begins. He depends upon no "key" letter whatever. This gives the trick a decided novelty, and leaves the "wise" spectators completely perplexed.

THE EFFECT

The performer introduces ten cards, each showing several letters of the alphabet. He gives these to a spectator; asks him to choose a letter and look through the cards one by one, to find which cards have the chosen letter printed on them.

The letters are in alphabetical arrangement; hence the spectator's task is a simple one. Each time he finds a card that bears his letter, he must lay that card upon the table, with its lettered side downward. That done, the spectator retains the extra cards.

The magician looks at the cards that are lying on the table. Although he has no opportunity to see the letters, for the blank sides of the cards are upward, he promptly names the letter that the spectator has mentally selected. The trick may be repeated.

THE METHOD

Ten cards are used; they are of two styles, oblong and square. When the proper cards are placed face down upon the table, you must look for the oblong ones. Call the first oblong card A.

If there are no other oblong cards, move to the square ones. Count the first square one A; the next B; then C, D, E. Wherever your mental count stops, you have the chosen letter. Thus one oblong (A) and two squares (A, B), would give B as the selection. One oblong (A) and four squares (A, B, C, D) give you D as the chosen letter.

If there are *two* oblong cards, count *five letters* for the first: A, B, C, D, E. Count the second oblong card as F. Then count the squares: F, G, H, I, J. Wherever the count stops, you have the chosen letters.

With *three* oblong cards, you must count five letters for the second, just as with the first. Thus the third oblong card will be K. Count the squares K, L, M, N, O. With *four* oblong cards, count five letters for the third. The fourth will be P. The square cards will run P, Q, R, S, T. With *five* oblong cards, count five letters for the fourth. The fifth will be U; the squares will run U, V, W, X, Y.

If there are no oblong cards, the chosen letter will be Z or the character &, which is known as ampersand. With no oblong cards present, three squares will signify Z; two will indicate &.

COMMENT

As a key to this trick, we may consider the following chart, which makes the system plain.

First Oblong: A   Squares: A, B, C, D, E
  (B, C, D, E)

Second Oblong: F   Squares: F, G, H, I, J
  (G, H, I, J)

Third Oblong: K   Squares: K, L, M, N, O
  (L, M, N, O)

Fourth Oblong: P   Squares: P, Q, R, S, T
  (Q, R, S, T)

Fifth Oblong: U   Squares: U, V, W, X, Y

No Oblongs: Three Squares: Z
             Two Squares: &

In brief, an oblong card gives you the "key letter" with which you start to count the squares. Should there be more than one oblong, each has the value of five squares, or letters, until you come to the last oblong, which thereupon becomes the "key letter" card. Count the squares beginning with that letter. The letter Z and the character Ampersand are merely left-overs, which must be considered as separate items.

This system has been arranged in units of five, to make the counting simple. All you have to know is the order of the alphabet. You can tell off the letters with the fingers of one hand. When you strike the final oblong card, your thumb will give its letter. Then start to tell off the square cards, beginning with that letter.

If the cards are laid in a pile upon the table, simply push them apart with one hand. Study the backs of the cards if you wish, or merely remember the number of each type and walk away, naming the letter afterward. With a little practice, you can learn to simply glance at the cards; then close your eyes and name the chosen letter after a period of mental concentration.

The necessary alphabet cards with their varied letter combinations will be found on one of the cardboard inserts bound with this volume. Cut out the cards to the exact size as shown and the required apparatus will be available for use.

PROGRAMS OF MAGIC

This section should be studied after you have learned to perform the tricks explained in the preceding pages of this volume.

It gives outlines for effective programs in each branch of magic and it also contains composite programs using tricks from various sections.

These programs will serve as an excellent guide for any entertainments that you decide to give, as special consideration has been given to the choice and arrangement of the different items.

Each program shows alternate items, separates those tricks that are too similar to be shown together, and has been designed to build up to an effective climax.

PROGRAMS IN THIS SECTION

Impromptu Magic

Table Magic

Card Magic

Oriental Magic

Mental Magic

Close-up Magic

Card Table Magic

Drawing Room Magic

Drawing Room Magic
(Without Card Tricks)

Formation of Programs

In presenting magic, one trick that is well done calls for another. Magical performances are received with anticipation; hence the audience's interest can always be sustained. Therefore, the formation of a program is important.

Tricks should be chosen that conform to the requirements of the particular occasion. The program should be long enough to satisfy the audience but it should finish while the interest is still at high level.

Specialized programs should be shorter than more general ones. Tricks should be chosen so that they form a coherent sequence. In addition, there are three distinct stages to every program that should always be remembered.

(1) THE OPENING.

Here you seek to gain immediate interest. You must use a trick that can be performed promptly, and which requires very little difficulty in its presentation.

(2) THE ROUTINE.

This is a series of tricks that form the body of the program. They should be varied; do not follow one trick with another of a very similar type, unless the second is stronger and more effective than the one before it.

(3) THE FINISH.

This should be a trick which produces a climax and can be presented almost as a mystery of its own. This leaves your audience puzzled at the conclusion of the entertainment.

The programs that appear on the following pages are arranged in chart form, offering choices of certain tricks. There is a program for each section of tricks described earlier in this volume; also composite programs that introduce varied types of magic.

Should longer programs be desired add additional tricks in the routine portion of the individual program.

In arranging programs from the charts, start from the top and follow the connecting lines to the bottom, choosing the alternate tricks that you prefer. Do not use unconnected tricks on the same program. You can vary your program by choosing a new combination from the chart, if you intend to give another performance before the same group of people.

PROGRAM ONE
(Impromptu Magic)

OPENING

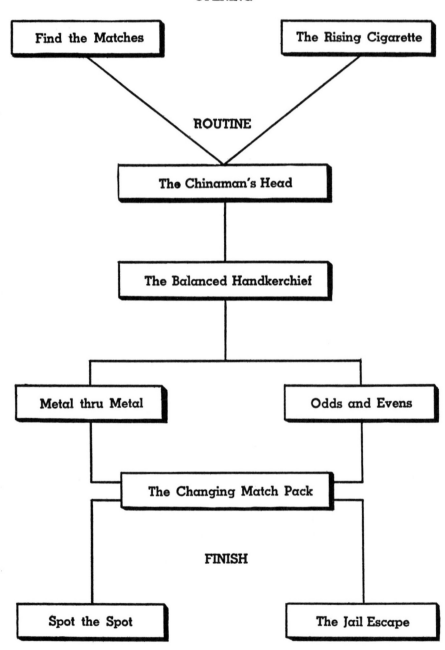

ROUTINE

PROGRAM TWO
(Table Magic)

OPENING

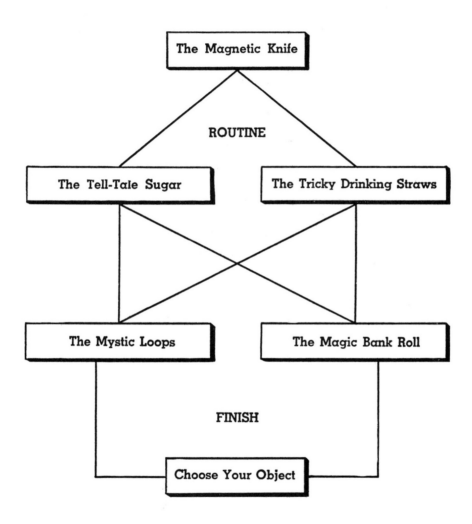

Note: This program can be extended by inserting supplementary items from the section on "Additional Magic." Such minor tricks, when used, should be placed between Items 2 and 3 in the program above.

PROGRAM THREE

(Card Magic)

OPENING

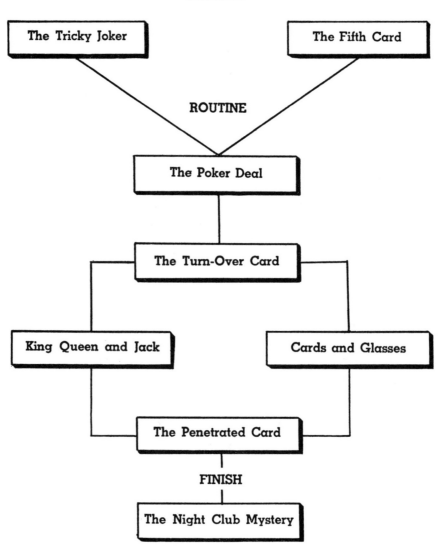

Note: The "Tricky Joker" requires the magician's own pack of cards (with extra joker). When such is not available, begin with the "Poker Deal" as opening. For the "Night Club Mystery" it is advisable to have an extra pack, with the cards set up. Otherwise a short delay is necessary. The "Penetrated Card" can serve as finish if the "Night Club Mystery" is not used.

PROGRAM FOUR

(Oriental Magic)

OPENING

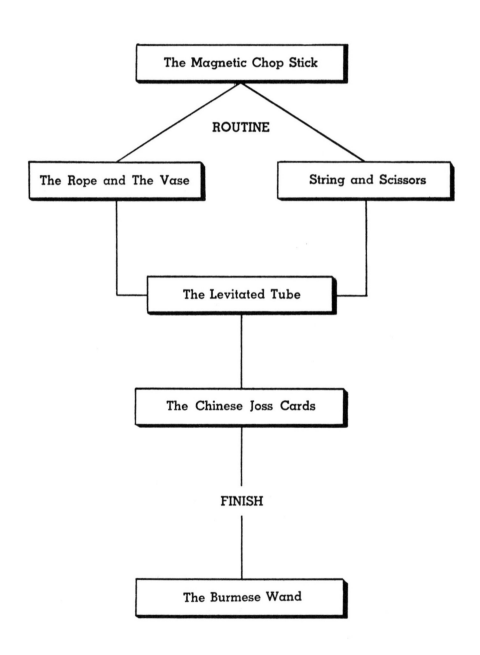

The Magnetic Chop Stick

ROUTINE

The Rope and The Vase

String and Scissors

The Levitated Tube

The Chinese Joss Cards

FINISH

The Burmese Wand

PROGRAM FIVE

(Mental Magic)

OPENING

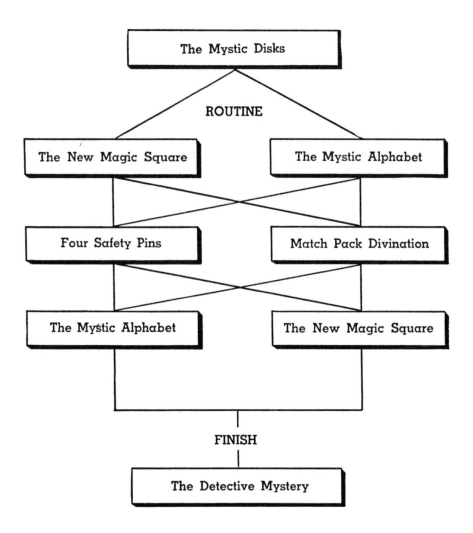

PROGRAM SIX

(Close-Up Magic)

OPENING

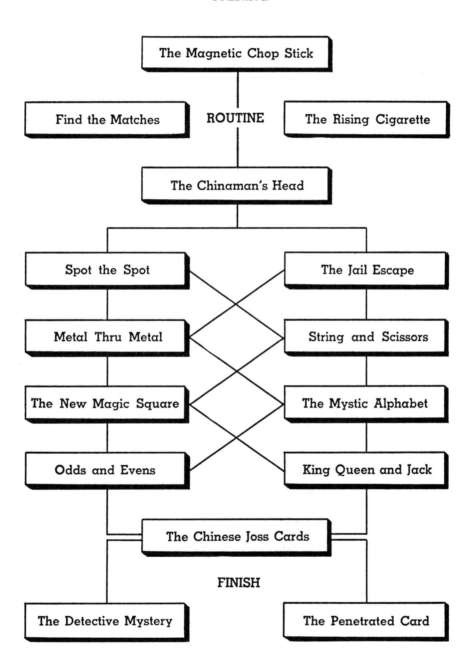

PROGRAM SEVEN
(Card Table Magic)

OPENING

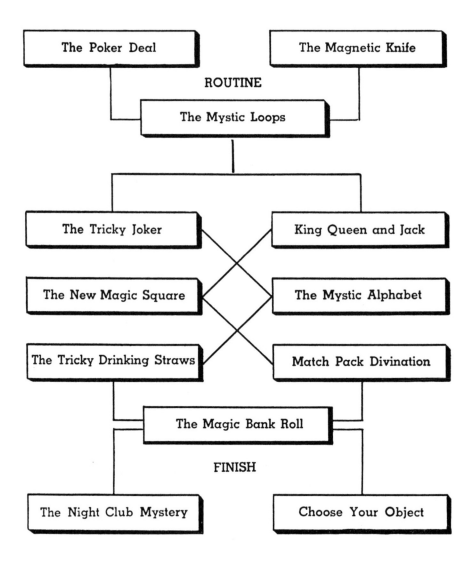

Note: An object other than a table knife may prove more suitable if the "Magnetic Knife" is used as opening for this program.

PROGRAM EIGHT
(Drawing Room Magic)

OPENING

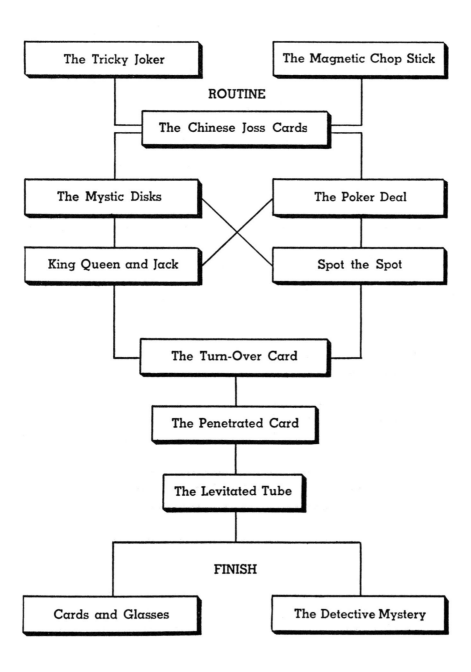

ROUTINE

FINISH

PROGRAM NINE

(Drawing Room Magic)

Without Card Tricks

OPENING

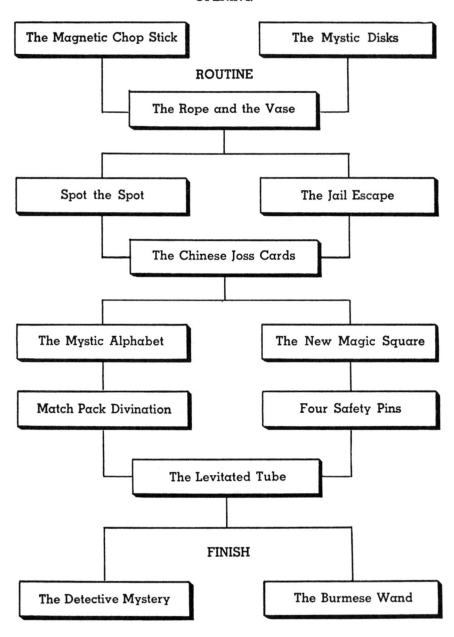

| The Magnetic Chop Stick | | The Mystic Disks |

ROUTINE

The Rope and the Vase

| Spot the Spot | | The Jail Escape |

The Chinese Joss Cards

| The Mystic Alphabet | | The New Magic Square |

| Match Pack Divination | | Four Safety Pins |

The Levitated Tube

FINISH

| The Detective Mystery | | The Burmese Wand |

ADDITIONAL MAGIC

After you have presented various programs of magic, you will find that you can acquire new tricks easily, once you know the secret and the general working method.

You will need new tricks, particularly if you perform before the same audiences, as many persons will remember your last program. It is good policy to introduce new effects, not only to add novelty to your performances, but also to keep people wondering what you will do next.

This section has been provided to supply the reader with additional tricks that can be used when required. With the knowledge gained through the study of the earlier sections, any one can easily adapt these supplementary tricks and add them to the proper programs.

A Classified Index will be found
at the end of the section.

Poker Chip Monte

EFFECT

Three poker chips are on the table. You mark an X on one with a pencil. Turn over the chip; move the three around. Ask some one to pick the marked chip. He guesses the wrong one.

METHOD

One of the chips is marked on the bottom. Moisten your thumb; mark a chip on the top and turn it over. Draw your thumb beneath, thus removing the mark. Another chip proves to be the marked one.

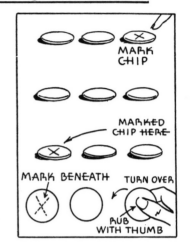

Returning Matches

EFFECT

Show a pack of paper matches, with the flap inserted behind the matches. Tear off the matches and pocket them. Open the match pack, with its back toward the spectators. Turn it around and show the matches returned.

METHOD

Insert the flap between two rows of matches. When you tear away the matches, only one layer goes. The rear row are the "returned" matches.

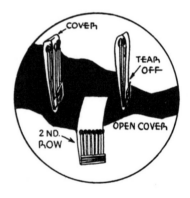

Vanishing Card

EFFECT

Three cards are held in a fan: a red spot card between two black ones. The cards are shuffled; the red card disappears. It arrives in the magician's pocket.

METHOD

Cut a small corner from an old playing card. This red corner is fanned between two black cards. The thumb hides the missing portion. Shuffle the cards, the corner drops into your hand. Drop it in your pocket when you reach for the real card.

Balanced Matches

EFFECT

A borrowed match pack is stood upon the table, upside down. It balances in that position. The pack is returned to the owner, with no clue to the trick.

METHOD

Open the pack to show the matches. Close it so the cover slides under one match. Stand the pack upside down, with the match toward yourself; the match supports the pack. Open the pack showing the matches as they were.

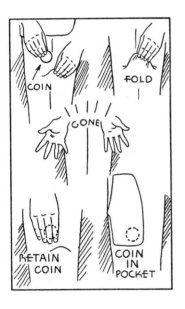

The Vanishing Coin

EFFECT

A coin is placed against the trousers. Cloth is folded upward, over the coin. Some one feels the coin in the fold. The fold is drawn down; the coin has vanished.

METHOD

Retain the coin with your fingers, when you draw the fold up over it. Carry the coin away in the hand. The coin felt by the spectator is a duplicate, in your trousers pocket.

The Talking Coin

EFFECT

A coin is set on top of an empty ginger ale bottle. Holding the bottle steady, you command the coin to talk. The coin rises and clicks. It repeats the action.

METHOD

Use a bottle that still contains a little liquid. Moisten the rim of the bottle, so the coin makes it air tight. The heat of your hand upon the bottle causes air expansion. This causes the coin to lift and drop back.

The Knotted Cigarette

EFFECT

The magician ties a cigarette into a knot.

METHOD

Flatten the cellophane wrapper from a cigarette pack. Lay a cigarette on it; roll the cellophane into a long tight tube, containing the cigarette. Tie the cellophane into a knot. The cigarette will form an actual knot inside it.

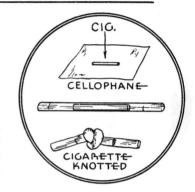

Naming the Number

EFFECT

A person takes a packet of ten cards; moves any number (not more than ten) from top to bottom, one by one. Receiving the packet, the magician names the number moved.

METHOD

Arrange the cards Ace, Two, etc. to Ten, from top to bottom. Receiving the packet, raise it to your forehead, glimpsing the bottom card. It tells the number moved. To repeat, remember the number previously noted. Subtract it from the new number. If the new number is larger than the old one, add 10 to the new number before you subtract.

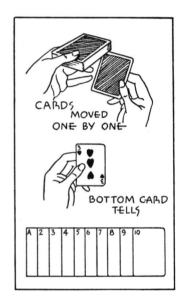

Deceptive Ice

EFFECT

The magician shows a glass of ice water; pours out some of the water. The water proves to be hot.

METHOD

The "ice" in the glass is crumpled cellophane. It will pass for ice at very close range. Simply add the cellophane to a glass of hot water. Show it as a glass of ice water.

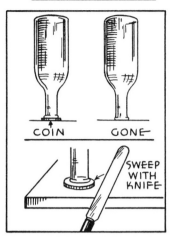

Knock Away Coin

EFFECT

The magician places a twenty-five cent piece upon the table. On it, he inverts a ginger ale bottle. He removes the coin without touching the bottle which remains standing.

METHOD

Lay the blade of a table-knife flat against the table. With a long, sweeping stroke, you can strike the coin away, leaving the bottle upright. Use a table with no cloth, and follow through with the knife stroke.

Brushing the Coin

EFFECT

A coin is placed on the flat palm. No one can brush it away. The magician removes the coin; brushes the palm himself. The coin returns.

METHOD

Since the palm is hollow, the sweeps of a whisk broom pass over the coin without disturbing it. After demonstrating this, secretly slide a coin upright in the whisk. Brush the empty palm slowly; the coin drops into it.

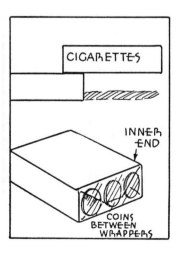

Gravity Defied

EFFECT

A pack of cigarettes is placed flat on the table; then drawn to the edge. The pack overbalances, but does not fall.

METHOD

Previously place a row of small coins in the bottom of the pack, under the outer wrapper. The added weight accounts for the defiance of gravity.

Predicted Totals

EFFECT

The magician shakes three dice in a cardboard pill box. He predicts their coming total, correctly.

METHOD

The pill box is reversible; either top or bottom can be the cover. Use dice just too large to turn inside the box. Drop three dice in the box; note their total and deduct it from 21. In shaking the box, turn it over. Name your new number. Removal of the bottom cover will show that total.

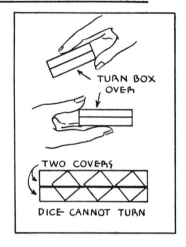

Restored String

EFFECT

A piece of paper is folded about the center of a string. Paper and string are cut; the string is restored.

METHOD

Use a thin string and a pair of loosened scissors. Cut the paper half through from one side; then cut clear across from the other side, following the slit. The paper will be clipped; but the string wedges between the scissor blades, and is uncut.

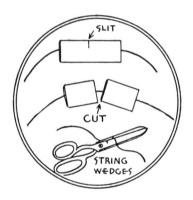

The Balanced Dice

EFFECT

The magician shows a pair of dice and balances one upon its corner.

METHOD

Place one of the dice with its five spot up. Set the corner of the other dice in the depressed center spot of the five. It will balance. Though a puzzle rather than a trick, this is an excellent table stunt.

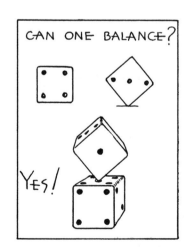

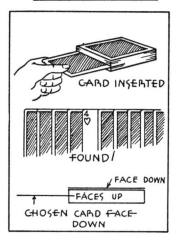

Half and Half

EFFECT

A shuffled pack is divided. A spectator takes a card from his portion and inserts it in the magician's half pack. Looking through his cards, the magician finds the chosen one.

METHOD

Turn your half of the pack face up; put the bottom card face down upon it. Hold the cards squared. You can find the chosen card after its insertion because it will be face up. Use a white-edged pack, and turn away when you look through your heap.

Tell the Color

EFFECT

The magician names the color of the match-heads in a pack of paper matches given to him behind his back.

METHOD

Use packs with red, blue, green matches. After receiving a pack, face the audience. Behind your back tear a match from the rear row of the pack; raise your hand to your forehead, bringing the match. Note the color of the head.

Divination Dice

EFFECT

The magician holds his hands behind his back. A pair of dice are placed in them; one dice in each hand. Spectators note the numbers that are up. The magician names those numbers.

METHOD

Face the audience momentarily and press your thumbs against the upper sides of the dice. The pressure leaves an impression. After returning the dice, a glance at each thumb will tell the numbers.

Six Goblets

EFFECT

Six goblets are placed in a row. The three at the left are full; the three at the right, empty. The trick is to touch or move one goblet only, yet make them alternately full and empty.

METHOD

Lift the middle of the three full glasses; pour its contents into the middle of the three empties. Replace the goblet that you lifted.

Cards and Hats

EFFECT

A card is selected. The pack is placed between two hats. The chosen card is slid between the brims. The pack is thoroughly shaken in the hats; yet the magician later discovers the chosen card.

METHOD

Bend the pack when you place it in a hat. Thus the chosen card can be distinguished by its straightness.

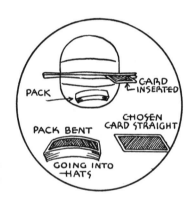

Chosen Dollar Bill

EFFECT

The serial number of a dollar bill is noted. The bill is wadded; dropped into a hat with other wadded ones. The magician picks out the chosen bill.

METHOD

Drop a tiny metal ball or small marble in the bill when you wad it. You can pick the bill by its weight, after the hat has been shaken.

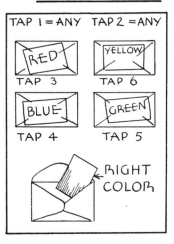

Four Colors

EFFECT

A person thinks of a primary color: red, yellow, green, or blue. He spells his color mentally as the magician taps four envelopes. The person announces the last letter; the magician opens the envelope. It contains a paper of the proper color.

METHOD

Have a different color paper in each envelope. Arrange the envelopes in the order: red, blue, green, yellow. Two taps at random; then in order. You will end on the right color.

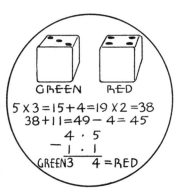

Red and Green

EFFECT

A mathematical stunt with dice. A person rolls a pair of dice; one red, the other green. He multiplies and adds as directed; his total tells the magician the numbers on the dice.

METHOD

Tell the person to multiply the green number by 5; to add the red number; double the total; then add 11 and subtract the red number. The total he then gives you will have two figures. Subtract 1 from the first figure for the green; 1 from the second for the red.

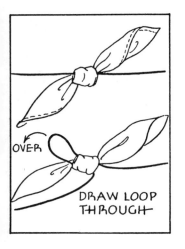

String and Handkerchief

EFFECT

The magician ties a handkerchief around a string. While the ends of the string are held, he frees the handkerchief without untying it.

METHOD

Push your finger through the loose knot, following the line of the handkerchief. Find the center of the string, draw it back through and over the end of the handkerchief. The handkerchief can be pulled clear of the string.

Card in Pocket

EFFECT

Four cards are dealt faces down. One is noted. The magician pockets one card; inserts the rest in a packet of a dozen. When the packet is riffled, selected card is gone. It is in the pocket.

METHOD

Have three *short* cards, their ends trimmed one-eighth inch. Have duplicates of these in your pocket. Deal one ordinary card with the shorts; it goes in your pocket. When the packet is riffled no short cards show. Whatever card is named as selected, you produce it.

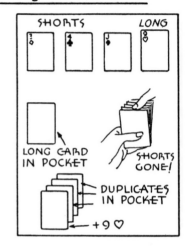

Balls of Yarn

EFFECT

Several small balls of yarn are given to spectators. One ball is dropped in the magician's hand, behind his back. He names the color of the yarn.

METHOD

Behind your back, break off a bit of the yarn. Return the ball; face the spectators; note the color of the tiny piece that you hold.

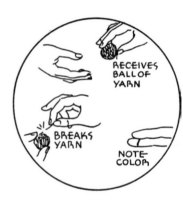

The Card Count

EFFECT

A pack is divided. A spectator notes a card; on to it, he counts cards to equal its value (as five cards for a five spot). He places these on his packet. The magician adds his cards; looks through the pack and finds the chosen one.

METHOD

Note the bottom card of your heap. Find it later; ignore the card below it. Then count one, two, etc. The chosen card will show on its count. In case two or three cards correspond to the count, ask suit or color of chosen one. That known, you can usually name it.

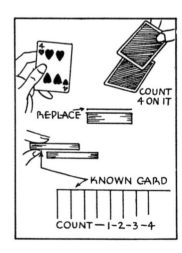

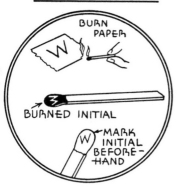

The Initial Trick

EFFECT

Some one writes an initial on a paper, which is burned. The initial appears on the match head.

METHOD

Pencil the initial on the head of a paper match, beforehand. Choose a person whose name begins with that letter. The initial will show on the head of the match after it is burned.

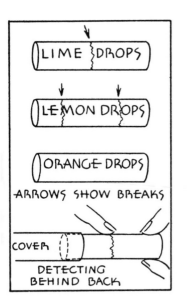

Mystic Candy Drops

EFFECT

The magician names the flavor of the candy drops in a pack which is given to him behind his back.

METHOD

Remove the wrappers from packs of lime and lemon drops. Break one pack in the center; the other in two places. Replace the wrapper. Also use an unprepared pack of orange drops. By sliding the wrapper off and on, you can tell the contents of any of the three packs.

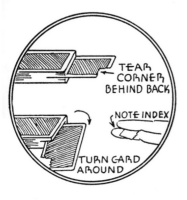

Guessing the Card

EFFECT

A card is drawn half way from a pack that the magician holds behind his back. Facing the spectators, the magician names the chosen card.

METHOD

Use an old pack. Tear a corner from the protruding card. When you face the audience, hold your fingers to your forehead, thus noting the torn index corner.

Cards in a Row

EFFECT

Borrowed playing cards are laid in a row. Some one moves cards from left to right, one card at a time. The magician tells the number moved, although he did not witness the action.

METHOD

Pick up a card by its extreme corner, digging it with the thumb nail, when demonstrating how to move the cards. Set this card at the left as "key." Its number from the right will be the number moved.

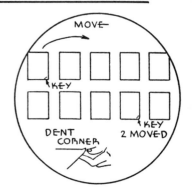

The Disappointed Match

EFFECT

A paper match is laid upon the left palm. The head of the match points away from the performer. The right forefinger is placed over the match; when it is lifted, the match points inward instead of outward.

METHOD

A paper match is previously split; the halves are pasted together, but with heads in opposite directions. This match can be shown with its head either way. A side motion of the forefinger imparts the necessary half turn.

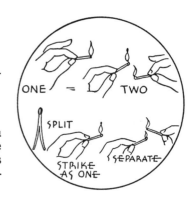

Multiplying Flame

EFFECT

A lighted match suddenly doubles, the magician showing two—one in each hand—instead of only one.

METHOD

Split a paper match from base to head. Hold it as a single match and strike it. In transferring it from one hand to another, separate the hands. The flame has loosened the sections; and each hand draws away carrying a separate "match" with its own flame.

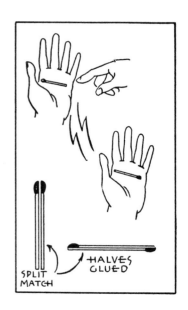

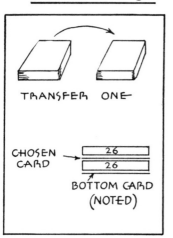

A Card Discovery

EFFECT

A shuffled pack is dealt in two heaps. Some one notes the top card of a heap, places it on the other heap, then adds the first heap. The magician takes the pack, allows it to be cut a few times. He then finds the selected card.

METHOD

Note the bottom card when you pick up the pack. Despite the single cuts that follow, the chosen card will remain just twenty-six from the one you noted. Use a pack of fifty-two cards.

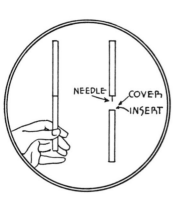

A Question of Balance

EFFECT

Two cigarettes are taken from a pack; one is balanced upright upon the other.

METHOD

Have a needle or pin projecting slightly from the end of one cigarette. The fingers hide the needle; in setting this cigarette in place, press the needle tip into the lower one. After removal, press the cigarette against the table, pushing the needle from view.

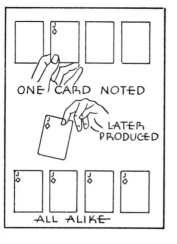

One From Four

EFFECT

Four cards are laid faces down. A person looks at one; the cards are mixed. The magician pockets them and produces the chosen card.

METHOD

Use four cards, all alike, taken from two pinochle decks. Only one card is noted; hence duplicates are not suspected. Pocket the four and bring out one. Have three extra cards, all different. Bring them out afterward, as if they were the other three original ones.

Index to Additional Magic Section

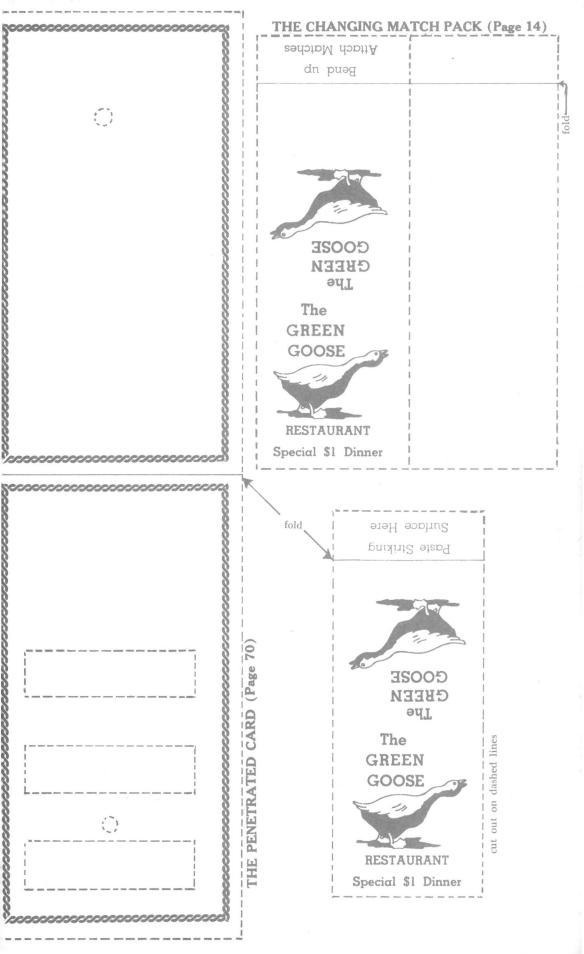

THE CHANGING MATCH PACK (Page 14)

Attach Matches

Bend up

fold

The
GREEN
GOOSE

RESTAURANT
Special $1 Dinner

THE PENETRATED CARD (Page 70)

fold

Paste Striking Surface Here

cut out on dashed lines

The
GREEN
GOOSE

RESTAURANT
Special $1 Dinner

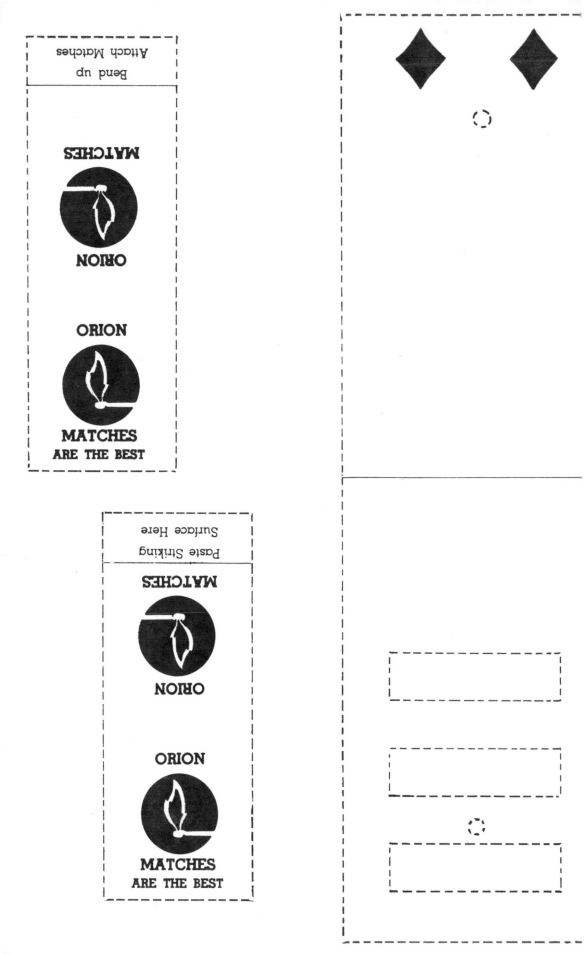

THE CHINESE JOSS CARDS (Page 94)

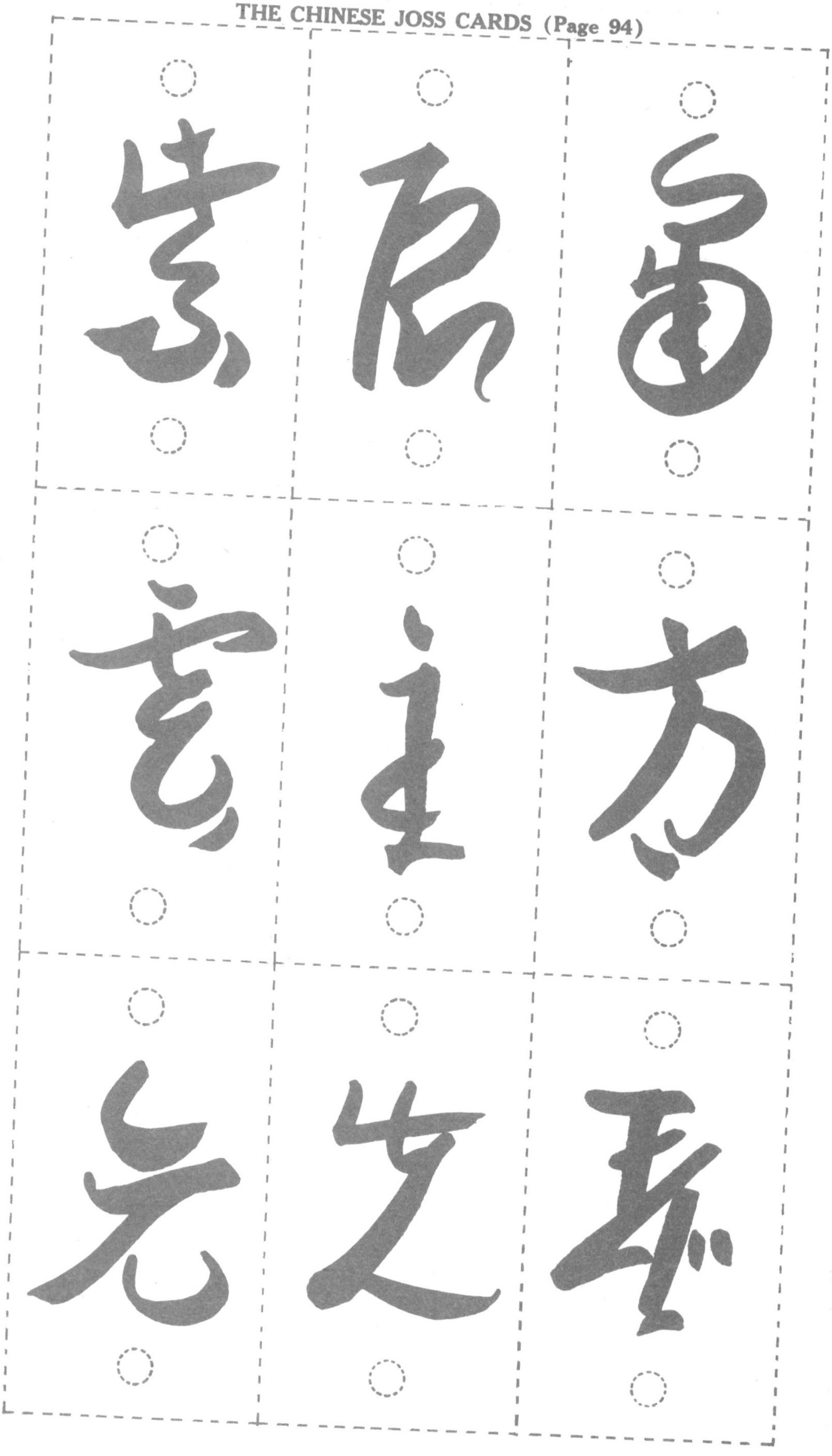

THE ICE BOX	THE GARAGE	THE AUTOMOBILE	THE SAFE
THE WATER TOWER	THE LAKE	THE CLOSET	THE BED
THE COAL BIN	THE STOVE	THE BASS DRUM	THE TREE
THE ATTIC	THE POLICE STATION	THE BAGGAGE CAR	THE THEATER
THE RESTAURANT	THE OFFICE	THE FERRIS WHEEL	THE BOWLING ALLEY
THE LION'S CAGE	THE PARKING LOT	THE BEAUTY PARLOR	THE ELEVATOR

A	C	G
I	L	M
P	Q	S
T	U	V
W	X	Y

B	E	F
G	L	N
O	Q	R
T	U	V
W	X	Y

D	H	J
K	L	O
P	Q	R
S	U	V
W	X	Y

F	I	K
M	N	O
P	R	S
T	U	V
W	X	Y

cut out on solid lines

A	B	D	E
H	J	K	N
O	P	R	T
W	X	Y	Z

H	J	K
M	N	P
Q	R	S
T	U	V
W	X	Y

B	C	D	E
I	J	L	M
O	Q	R	S
T	W	Y	Z

C	E	F	H
I	J	M	N
O	R	S	T
W	X	Y	Z

C	D	E	G
I	J	L	N
O	Q	S	T
V	X	Y	&

D	E	G	H
I	J	M	N
O	S	T	U
V	X	Y	&

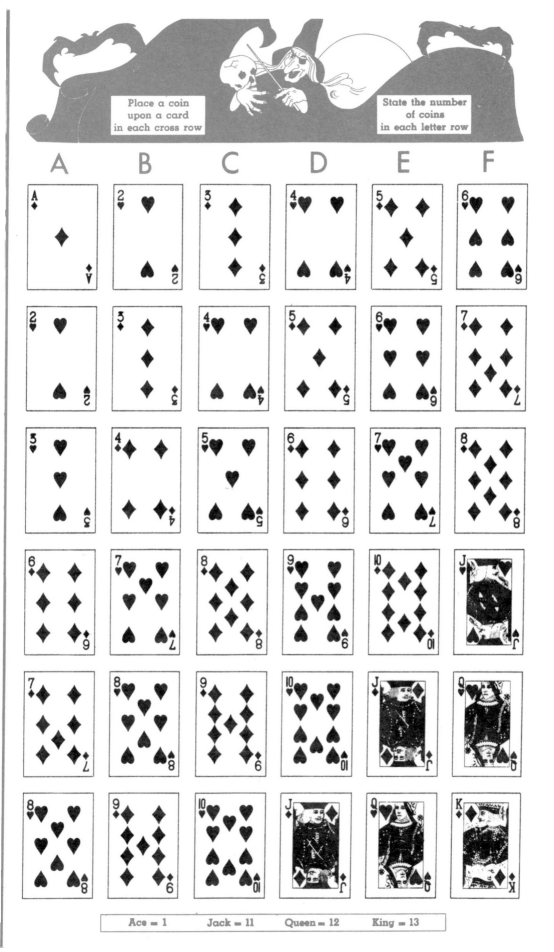

THE FALSE TEETH	THE GUM DROPS	THE POISON	THE REVOLVER
THE KNIFE	THE BODY	THE FINGER PRINTS	THE WILL
THE MURDERER	THE GLASS EYE	THE JEWELS	THE GORILLA
THE BLOOD STAINS	THE MILLION DOLLARS	THE MAP	THE OIL CAN
THE NEEDLE	THE RATTLE SNAKE	THE HAIR PIN	THE INFANT
THE POLICEMAN	THE CANNON BALL	THE CHEESE	THE DYNAMITE

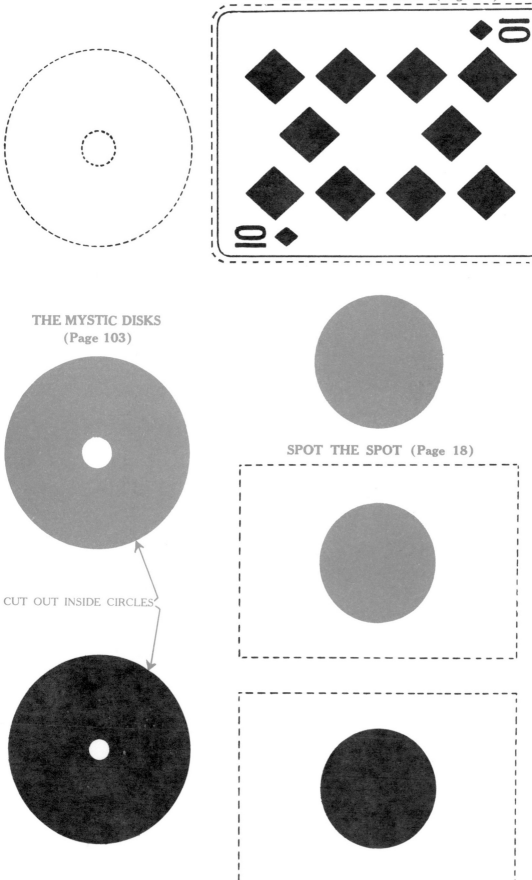

CARDS AND GLASSES (Page 74)

THE MYSTIC DISKS
(Page 103)

SPOT THE SPOT (Page 18)

CUT OUT INSIDE CIRCLES

cut out on dashed lines

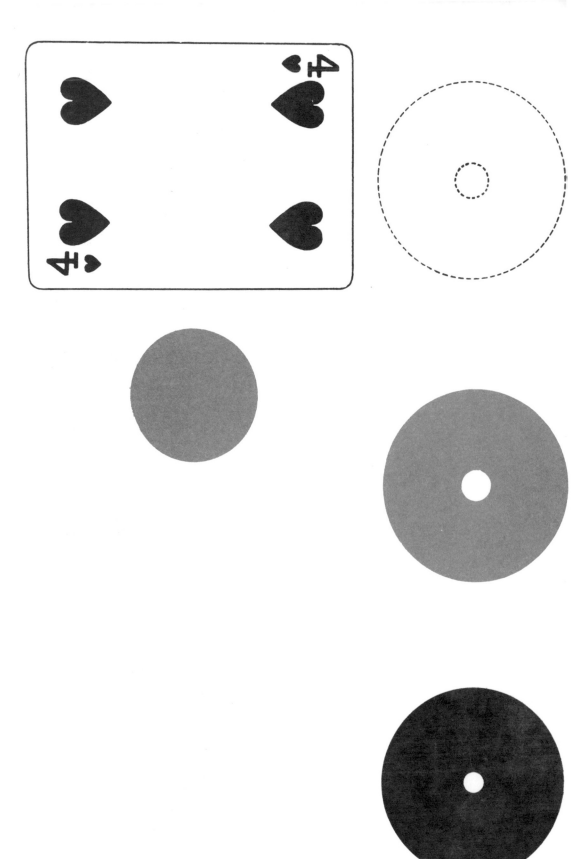

CUT OUT BOXES